The Small Business Troubleshooter

By
Roger Fritz

CAREER PRESS
3 Tice Road
P.O. Box 687
Franklin Lakes, NJ 07417
1-800-CAREER-1
201-848-0310 (NJ and outside U.S.)
FAX: 201-848-1727

THE SMALL BUSINESS TROUBLESHOOTER
ISBN 1-56414-191-8, $16.99
Cover design by The Gottry Communications Group, Inc.
Printed in the U.S.A. by Book-mart Press

To order this title by mail, please include price as noted above, $2.50 handling per order, and $1.00 for each book ordered. Send to: Career Press, Inc., 3 Tice Road., P.O. Box 687, Franklin Lakes, NJ 07417.

Or call toll-free 1-800-CAREER-1 (Canada: 201-848-0310) to order using VISA or MasterCard, or for further information on books from Career Press.

Library of Congress Cataloging-in-Publication Data

Fritz, Roger
   The small business troubleshooter / by Roger Fritz.
      p.   cm.
   Includes index.
   ISBN 1-56414-191-8 (pbk.)
   1. Small business--Management--Handbooks, manuals, etc.
   2. Problem solving--Handbooks, manuals, etc.   I. Title.
HD62.7.F76   1995
658.02'2--dc20   95-17521
                                                                         CIP

Dedication

To Dick Sanford, founder and chairman of Intelligent Electronics, Inc., who combines compassion with an ability to create incentives, growth strategies, motivation and mutual benefit better than anyone I have known.

Acknowledgments

The two keys to this project were: 1) determining the categories of problems to be featured (so that busy people *could* use them), and 2) distilling the recommendations (so that busy people *would* use them). In both of these efforts, Don Young was invaluable. His special talents are greatly appreciated.

I am also grateful to the scores of my clients, past and present, whose real-life experiences have provided the foundation on which this book was built. Thanks for the opportunity and the challenge.

Contents

Instant Troubleshooter

Pinpoint solutions to your problems at a glance. The numbers listed correspond to the numbers of the troubleshooter problems in the book.

Managing yourself

Motivating yourself: 16, 147

Getting more done: 4-5, 46, 91, 146

Getting organized: 18, 81, 141

Getting more out of meetings: 94-96, 98-99

Learning to delegate: 20, 79-80, 90, 146

Listening to others: 9, 69, 82-86

Managing teams: 50-53

Managing uncertainty: 8, 24, 140

Managing and motivating people

Hiring and training new people: 6, 39-41, 44-46, 56, 66, 70

Retaining and motivating key staff: 20, 66-68, 70-73

Paying and promoting employees: 43, 74-78

Dealing with problem employees: 54-55, 60, 65

Releasing and laying off employees: 60-61, 65

Managing people: 9, 19-20, 25-26, 49, 69, 91

Managing teams: 50-53

Managing the plant: 47-48

Mediating conflicts: 26, 57-59, 64

Communicating with staff: 62, 72, 87

Gaining or losing partners: 89, 136, 138-139

Working with family members: 136

Managing money

Expanding products, markets and customer base

Creating your future

Preface

Experience has taught me it is not the lack of lightning-bolt innovative ideas that breaks you, but the relentless pressures of unsolved problems.

Nagging troubles are business killers. They hobble the owners, cripple the executives, neutralize the managers and stymie the employees. Identifying the worst ones and deciding how to deal with them is more than half the battle. *The Small Business Troubleshooter* diagnoses and provides the prescription for 152 ills that can befall the small business owner.

Time after time, these prescriptions cut to the core of an issue and provide one or more practical, workable recommendations, ideas or solutions.

The best advice I can give: Keep it handy!

Joseph A. Piscopo,
founder and chairman of Pansophic Systems

Introduction

The key to success in business lies not in inspiration, but in recovery. Those who bounce back make it. Those who don't know how to react to trouble fall behind and fail.

Every business has problems. Survival requires solving problems as they arise. Growth requires converting those solutions into future opportunities.

This book gives you a head start by:

1. Anticipating the core problems that will drag you down.

2. Providing either specific or optional solutions that will enable you to move forward.

Not a small-business syndrome

As we've learned recently, large multinational corporations are scarcely more secure than their smaller brethren. For all of their glorious history, tremendous sales volume, multibillion-dollar budgets, instant name recognition, thousands of employees, enormous bank accounts and enviable reputations, they have very serious problems.

For example, in case you've forgotten:

- Addressograph-Multigraph Corporation ignored the value of R&D, refused to recognize the threat posed by emerging technologies and allowed itself to become incredibly top-heavy before it finally slipped into bankruptcy. When the company ultimately did emerge from court control, it reappeared as the dramatically slimmed-down AM International.

- Chrysler Corporation was hit by a terrible cash crisis, right in the midst of a recession. The company might have gone under had it not been for substantial financial support provided by the federal government.

- International Harvester was so badly crippled by a labor strike in 1979 that it survives today only as a shell of the industrial giant it once was.
- IBM, which once had a virtual monopoly on the explosive computer business, has faced horrendous business problems in recent years.
- And remember the problems at General Motors, Sears and the nation's savings-and-loan industry, which all but collapsed during the late 1980s, sweeping hundreds of thousands of depositors along with it.

To make a business grow, its leaders must grow. Usually trouble is caused not by a flaw in the original business plan or in the assumptions on which the plan was based. Rather, it comes from other factors, such as the introduction of new technology, increased competition, the fickle mood of the market or the state of the local or national economy.

Those who create change often find themselves alone and exposed.

Know when it's time to take action

Business problems are not unique to your business...or your market...or your industry. Everybody has them. The difference is many people do not have the good judgment to seek help, as you are doing now. But outsiders can do only so much. You must do the most difficult part yourself:

1. Admit that you need help.
2. Determine the nature of the problem and the type of help that is needed.
3. Get whatever help is necessary.
4. Most of all, take prompt action to solve the problem once you have determined what needs to be done.

In bad times as well as in good, the person who heads a business must learn to rely on the company's strengths and must learn from mistakes, rather than dwell upon them after they've been resolved. And the most important lesson of all is to never repeat the same mistake.

In this book, we address critical problems. It is directed primarily to the owners of small businesses—that is, those who employ between six and 50 people, with perhaps $10 million a year in sales.

What's in a word?

As used here, the word *entrepreneur* refers to the founder of a small business, regardless of its size or type; the word *product* is used to signify either product or service, unless it is specifically stated otherwise in the text. Most of the topics discussed here have less to do with *what* you sell than with *how* to run your business.

For quick and easy reference we have followed a simple format for each topic:

PROBLEM: What is wrong.

DIAGNOSIS: What must be recognized to analyze causes.

PRESCRIPTION: What should be done.

Improvement comes only when these three steps are taken. When this happens you will be amazed how often you can be your own troubleshooter...and how accurate and effective your results will be.

Chapter 1

Where are you headed?

1. The importance of planning

PROBLEM: Too often you have the feeling that you're flying by the seat of your pants or working day-to-day without any well-conceived idea of what you ought to be doing. As a result, you often feel that you're doing things to keep busy, but not actually making progress toward your long-range goals.

DIAGNOSIS: From the very beginning, your business needs a well-defined plan, designed to keep you on course and prevent you from straying too far afield. Good intentions don't get the job done. Like a road map, a solid business plan will help guide you to where you want to go.

A business plan actually serves six key functions:

- It communicates your ideas, research and plans throughout the organization.

- It provides essential information for potential sources of funding, such as prospective partners or bankers.

- It provides the framework on which to build your business.

- It provides a means for managing your business.

- It provides a yardstick for measuring the company's progress.

- It provides a way to evaluate change, not only in your business, but in your industry, your market and yourself.

PRESCRIPTION: Prepare a detailed business plan, which entails:

Defining your goals

- ➲ Be brief.
- ➲ Be specific.
- ➲ Put them in writing.
- ➲ Make sure they are measurable.

Collecting all of the relevant data

- ➲ Get input from internal and external sources.
- ➲ Tap customers, suppliers, bankers and advisers.
- ➲ Consult the library, applicable trade associations, the chamber of commerce, colleges and universities.
- ➲ If necessary, consult private consultants such as market research firms.

Developing the plan

- ➲ Select and train new employees, as needed.
- ➲ Acquire new equipment, if necessary.
- ➲ Form new business relationships, if indicated.
- ➲ Determine how to finance the plan.

Implementing the plan

- ➲ Set the plan in motion by delegating key assignments.
- ➲ Follow up when necessary.
- ➲ Revise the plan as needed.

2. Preparing your business plan

PROBLEM: You recognize the need for a sound business plan but you haven't the foggiest notion as to what is involved or how to go about creating one.

DIAGNOSIS: Planning is problem-solving. To be effective, it must:

- Be flexible enough to adapt as circumstances change.
- Reflect reality.
- Reflect the skills and knowledge of those who must carry it out.
- State specific ways in which to achieve the company's goals and objectives.
- Be communicated—and perhaps explained—to those who ultimately must implement it.

PRESCRIPTION: Design your business plan around these elements:

Your business concept

- ➲ What is your business idea?
- ➲ Why do you think it will work?
- ➲ How does it fit into the marketplace?
- ➲ How do you perceive the future prospects?
- ➲ How will startup details be handled?
  - Establishing an office.
- ➲ How will you hire employees?
  - Acquiring licenses.
  - Meeting other regulations and requirements.
  - Acquiring insurance(s).
- ➲ How will you run the company on a day-to-day basis?
  - Business hours.
  - Billing procedures.
  - Bookkeeping systems.
  - Quality assurance safeguards.
- ➲ Will the company be a proprietorship, a partnership or a corporation?
- ➲ Who else will be involved in the decision-making process?

Your product (or service)

- ➲ What do you plan to sell?
- ➲ What advantages will help to sell it to a customer?
- ➲ What disadvantages does it have and how can they be overcome?
- ➲ How will your product or idea be protected—patent, copyright, protected logo?
- ➲ If you have test data, attach it.
- ➲ Attach any appropriate photographs or illustrations.

Your market

- ➲ Where will you locate your business? Why?
- ➲ Who are your customers?
- ➲ Who are your competitors?
- ➲ Is the industry growing or declining?

➲ What is happening or is expected to happen that will affect your business?

➲ What is your special place in the market?

Your marketing strategy

➲ What will you name your business?

➲ How will your product be sold?

➲ What will your pricing strategy be?

➲ How do you propose to make contact with your customers?

➲ Why will your customers buy your product?

➲ How successful are your competitors? Why?

➲ What are your competitors' weaknesses?

➲ Will your business fill a need created by a competitor's weakness?

➲ Attach estimated sales and market share projections for each of the first three years.

Your production strategy

➲ How, where and by whom will your product be produced?

➲ What supplies will you require? Do you have a source?

➲ What volume of production do you anticipate? How does this compare with the estimated sales and market share projections you provided in marketing strategy?

Your human resources

➲ Will you have any supporting advisers? Who will they be, and what are their qualifications?

➲ How many employees will you need?

➲ What skills and/or training will your employees need?

➲ When will these employees be added to the company?

➲ If appropriate, include an organization chart.

Your financial needs

➲ How much money do you need?

➲ How much money do you have?

➲ Where will you get additional funding that may be needed?

➲ When will your first revenues begin to come in?

➲ How do you expect to increase your revenues—and your profits—over a period of time?

➲ If the business is a startup, attach your personal financial statement to the plan; if it is an established business, attach the *business* financial statement to it.

3. Goals: a sense of direction

PROBLEM: The business *seems* to be doing well, but many of the key people often appear to wander about in a daze, not knowing what to do next.

DIAGNOSIS: You have failed to establish—and communicate—a solid set of goals by which to achieve the company's basic business objectives.

PRESCRIPTION: Success and failure stem from the same source: goals. If there is no goal—no "target"—you cannot tell if you are progressing as you should or not.

Goals should never be set in stone; they should be simple guidelines to help you and your personnel stay on the right path. They should not be rigid and inflexible, nor should they ever be considered ends unto themselves.

It is all right to pursue several goals simultaneously, as long as you don't try to take on too much at one time.

Goals should be specific, and they should be measurable. They should identify *what* you are after, not *how* you propose to get there. Most of all, your goals should always be practical, workable—and attainable. Try to follow these guidelines:

A good goal must ensure improvement

➲ Will it be a challenge to your employees?
➲ In pursuing the goal, will your employees have to overcome problems and capitalize on opportunities?
➲ Once the goal has been reached, will it make someone's job easier, better, more productive or more profitable?
➲ Will your employees feel good about themselves after attaining their goal?

A good goal must be specific

➲ Does the goal identify *exactly* what you are after?
➲ Can your employees measure where they began, how far they have to go and how much they achieved in the interim?

➡ Have you set a series of dates for reaching certain milestones? And for when the goal ultimately should be reached?

A good goal must be realistic

➡ Are you sure your goal is attainable—something that is *possible* to achieve, not something it would merely be *nice* to achieve?

➡ Have you allowed sufficient time for your employees to attain your goal? Imposing impossible deadlines will discourage people rather than energize them. If reaching your ultimate goal will take too long, perhaps it would be wise to set up *lesser* goals along the way that can be achieved in a more reasonable span of time.

➡ Have you estimated the cost of the project and made the necessary funds available? If the costs are greater than the benefits, perhaps you would be wise to modify your goal.

4. Business or *busyness*?

PROBLEM: The company keeps hiring new employees and all appear to be busy, but productivity and profitability are going down.

DIAGNOSIS: You must learn the difference between activity and results, between efficiency and effectiveness.

PRESCRIPTION: Activities are the *means* to an end; results are what you're after. Efficiency is doing things right; effectiveness is doing the *right* things right. Having come to that realization:

➡ Review your work flow.

➡ Review the job descriptions of your employees. See if they can't be tightened up. Rewrite them, if necessary.

➡ Simplify your systems and procedures. Maybe there are too many steps in getting your work from Point A to Point B.

➡ Combine the assignments of your employees, taking work away from the *least* capable individuals and giving it to the *most* capable.

➡ Eliminate as many of the less-competent employees as you can. If increasing their workload seems to irritate the remaining employees, consider giving them a modest raise; paying a few good people a little bit more may cost you less than paying two people to do the work of one.

While you are doing all of this, keep your eye on the work flow to be sure you're not eliminating the wrong tasks, and watch your level of productivity to be sure that it either stays level or increases—then see if your profitability doesn't improve tremendously.

A caution: When you cut back on personnel, be sure you cut back enough. The tendency is to *under*cut, rather than to *over*cut.

5. Simplifying work procedures

PROBLEM: Too much time is being spent relocating materials, shuffling paperwork, filling out forms, holding meetings and doing other nonproductive work.

DIAGNOSIS: Someone must find ways to improve work procedures. If you are the CEO and aren't doing this, it's probably because you introduced the procedure in the first place and now you're probably too busy to spend time on such "details." Besides, you may be too far removed from the root of the problems to be of much help.

PRESCRIPTION: Create a renewal team consisting of your best people and assign them to study each operation within the company: product planning, marketing and sales, manufacturing (if applicable), cost control, and quality assurance.

➲ Let them know that you are interested in hearing about every conceivable improvement, no matter how insignificant it might seem at first.

➲ Let them know that there are no sacred cows, and assure them that every suggestion will be seriously and thoroughly considered.

➲ Give them a reasonable timetable in which to complete their work and all of the resources they will need to do it properly.

6. Preparing your operations manual

PROBLEM: The company is innovative and takes pride in doing things its own way. That has been one of its strengths. It has helped the firm improve productivity, reduce cost and, as a result, increase profits.

But every time a new employee comes aboard, it's like going back to square one. The way the new employee has done things in the past no longer applies, and he or she doesn't know your procedures. It often takes months before the new employee can be trained and brought up to speed.

DIAGNOSIS: It sounds like your company needs a comprehensive manual of operations. The more innovative a company is, the more valuable such a manual can be, but even in a traditional environment, a manual of operations can do a great deal to identify the company's objectives and its chosen methods for reaching them. Among the benefits a manual provides:

- It establishes a single-source reference to company policies and procedures. No more relying on memory or interpretation.

- It makes administrative and human relations policies more consistent and even-handed.

- It defines lines of authority and distributes responsibility more clearly.

- It encourages greater objectivity in decision-making by helping to eliminate emotional or "gut" decisions.

- It encourages continuity of management style through the company.

- It presents standard forms and reporting formats, which encourages uniformity in reporting and helps reduce paperwork.

- It helps identify problems before they arise.

- It is a natural training tool for new employees.

PRESCRIPTION: A comprehensive operations manual should consist of 10 sections, more or less.

Section 1: Introduction

- ➲ States the purpose of the manual.
- ➲ Gives the history of the company.
- ➲ Presents the philosophy and objectives of the company.
- ➲ Describes the company's products/services.
- ➲ Discusses the economics of the business.

Section 2: Organization chart

- ➲ Identifies who reports to whom.
- ➲ Includes job descriptions.
- ➲ Describes the company's facilities.
- ➲ Outlines the purpose of each department and division.

Section 3: General employee information

- ⮑ Attitude toward customers, suppliers, other employees.
- ⮑ Telephone procedures.
- ⮑ Handling visitors.
- ⮑ Housekeeping policies.

Section 4: Human resources

- ⮑ Hiring practices.
- ⮑ Employee forms:
  - • Employment applications.
  - • Contracts.
  - • Tax forms.
- ⮑ Frequency and method of paying employees.
- ⮑ Payroll deductions.
- ⮑ Frequency of salary reviews.
- ⮑ Benefits:
  - • Paid by the company.
  - • Contributory.
- ⮑ Advancement opportunities.
- ⮑ Vacations.
- ⮑ Holidays.
- ⮑ Scheduling.
- ⮑ Hours.
- ⮑ Overtime.
- ⮑ Coffee and lunch breaks.
- ⮑ Dress code.
- ⮑ Personal behavior.
- ⮑ Outside employment.
- ⮑ Labor laws.
- ⮑ Reprimands.

Section 5: Products/services

- ⮑ Customer relations.
- ⮑ Supplier relations.
- ⮑ Sales procedures.

Section 6: Reports and records

- ➲ Administrative procedures.
- ➲ Ensuring accountability.
- ➲ Billings.
- ➲ Samples of all forms.
- ➲ Purpose of all forms.
- ➲ Paperwork flow chart.
- ➲ Summary of deadlines and due dates.

Section 7: Safety and security

- ➲ Protection of the premises.
- ➲ Personal security.
- ➲ Protection of company's assets.
- ➲ Handling of confidential information.

Section 8: Emergencies

- ➲ Dealing with accidents.
- ➲ What to do if there's a fire.
- ➲ Power failures.
- ➲ Robberies.
- ➲ Thefts.
- ➲ Emergency telephone numbers.

Section 9: Maintenance and repair

- ➲ Handling equipment.
- ➲ Property damage or loss.
- ➲ Who authorizes repairs.
- ➲ Telephones.
- ➲ Service people.
- ➲ Trash removal.
- ➲ Key control.

Section 10: Legal matters

- ➲ Compliance with local, state and federal laws.
- ➲ Handling of regulatory agencies.
- ➲ Inspections.
- ➲ Record-keeping requirements.

A three-ring loose-leaf binder makes an excellent repository for this material. Referring to and updating the manual are easier when this sort of binder is used.

Operations manuals should always be considered flexible and open to improvement, providing there's an established authority assigned to approve all changes. The entire manual should be reviewed at least once a year.

7. Maintaining confidence

PROBLEM: The news has been bad for six months. You have missed your sales and profit targets for two straight quarters, your largest customer cut his order by 50 percent and your landlord won't renew your lease. Your discouragement is beginning to show.

DIAGNOSIS: Organizations take on the characteristics of their owners and leaders. When people at the top lose their confidence, employees lose confidence. When people at the top don't plan, employees don't plan.

PRESCRIPTION: In my book, *Nobody Gets Rich Working for Somebody Else,* I devote a chapter to "Managing Yourself...and Your Business." In it, I list a number of things self-confident leaders do and a number of things they do not do.

For example, confidence becomes infectious and spreads throughout the work force when you:

➲ Are consistently observed putting your time to good use.

➲ Are flexible in your thinking and try new things.

➲ Channel work toward people's strengths.

➲ Reward and retain only the best performers.

You will also notice self-confidence developing in your people when you avoid these stifling temptations:

➲ Don't dwell on *who* caused a failure, but on *what* caused the failure and *why*.

➲ Don't clutter your organization with deadwood, but replace nonperforming individuals with competent, enthusiastic, well-motivated people.

⊃ Don't promote on the basis of seniority, but on the basis of performance.

⊃ Don't shackle your employees with a lot of unimportant rules, regulations and conditions.

⊃ Don't dominate the decision-making process, but welcome and encourage the input of those who do the work.

⊃ Don't set unrealistic goals.

Chapter 2

Minimizing risk

8. Living with risk

PROBLEM: You've decided the company is ready to become more aggressive in the expansion of its facilities, in developing new products and in entering new markets. You have agreed to these changes on the advice of your most valued advisers, but you are a conservative individual. How do you handle the anxiety of living with risk?

DIAGNOSIS: Roberto Goizueta, chairman of Coca-Cola, once said: "If you take risks, you may still fail; but if you do not take risks, you will surely fail. The greatest risk of all is to do nothing."

PRESCRIPTION: Recognize that few things in life come with a guarantee. A certain level of risk is unavoidable. Overly cautious businesspeople waste a lot of their financial and human resources on simply trying to avoid risk. They would be better advised to learn how to minimize the adverse effects of risk.

- ⊃ Establish cut-off points to indicate the limits beyond which you will not go.
- ⊃ Maintain control by delegating risk and responsibility, rather than simply exercising your authority.
- ⊃ If you encounter failure, take the responsibility for it, decide what went wrong and take the necessary corrective steps.
- ⊃ Obtain the necessary financial and human resources to deal with risk by being willing to share the potential rewards with others.
- ⊃ Reduce the intellectual and financial sides of risk by using other people's brains and other people's money.
- ⊃ *Never* adopt the "I'll make this work if it kills me" attitude, or countenance it in others.

Instead of trying to avoid it, seek out risk. Weigh the possibilities for gains and losses. And when the odds seem to be in your favor, move boldly ahead. As they say in the sports field: "No pain, no gain."

9. How to test an idea

PROBLEM: Your people keep flooding you with ideas, but how can you tell if an idea is a good one or a bad one without running the risk of wasting time, wasting money and doing some permanent damage to the business?

DIAGNOSIS: There are some questions you can use to test the value of your ideas.

PRESCRIPTION: Answers to these questions will serve as a guide to the worth of a new idea:

- If the idea were fully implemented, what would be the ultimate contribution to the company's performance?
- Does the idea have application in any other area of the business?
- Does the idea conflict with the objectives of any group within the company?
- Will the idea help you to reach your objectives?
- Is anything standing in the way of implementing the idea?
- If any impediments stand in the way of implementing the idea, can they be easily eliminated?
- Do you have the sole authority to implement the idea or do you need to check with accounting or the legal department?
- Can you sell the idea to the employees?
- Do you have the resources to implement the idea without impairing any of your other objectives?
- If you need additional resources, do you know where to get them?

10. When your image is tarnished

PROBLEM: Ten years ago, who could possibly have guessed that the previously unassailable image of the American health care industry would become tarnished by a dramatic change in public perception? Yet that's exactly what happened shortly after the presidential election in 1992 and the subsequent efforts to "reform" health care at the federal level.

Similarly, changing market conditions, environmental concerns and a number of other factors have been altering the public perception of many other industries of late.

What can you do if it should happen to you?

DIAGNOSIS: Do not take such assaults lightly. Remember what has happened to the American auto makers, the tobacco industry, the lumber industry, the dairy industry, the apple growers and numerous other businesses that once were considered as safe and secure as God and country, only to experience some sudden and traumatic assault.

When such assaults develop, they often are extremely hostile, and they can reach national or international proportions if they should capture the attention of some aggressive media.

At the first hint of an impending problem, a prudent company will take swift and positive action.

PRESCRIPTION: When your image is at stake, you cannot afford to take a passive position, hoping that this too will disappear. There is too much at stake to take that gamble.

You should:

➲ Take personal charge of the situation. It's too important to delegate.

➲ Act promptly. Time is an extremely important factor. You need to get on top of the situation *before* it gets out of hand. Once a story has been allowed to spread—even if the information is false—it is doubly hard to regain control. (To cite a common example: We *always* hear when someone is charged with a crime, but *seldom* hear if the charge is later dropped.)

➲ Be accessible to anyone who can provide useful information. You need to know as much as possible as quickly as possible.

➲ Tell the media—and any other important parties that may be involved in the situation—that you will tell them whatever they want to know. If the information isn't immediately available, tell them that you will get it to them as quickly as possible, and then *do* it.

➲ Set up a command post. Recruit whatever assistance you need—public relations, legal, financial, marketing, engineering. Be sure that they are thoroughly briefed on what is going on and what the company's position is.

- ⮑ Ask your legal counsel to identify the danger points and the potential effects of litigation. Learn what can and should be said and done, and what words and acts should be carefully avoided. Be sure everyone on your team understands these considerations, but do not overreact to the various legal concerns that may be expressed.

- ⮑ Open the lines of communication, both inside and outside the company. Set up dedicated telephone lines for dealing with those who may be involved in the situation.

- ⮑ Set up a spokesperson to deal with the media and the public. This individual should be pleasant, but tough-minded.

- ⮑ Monitor the media to learn the latest developments in the situation.

- ⮑ Pinpoint the problem and its cause. Someone started the brouhaha and for a reason. Who was it? Why did they attack you? And what do they hope to gain? Why has the issue suddenly jumped into prominence?

- ⮑ Use the telephone to canvass your customers, suppliers and any others who may be influenced by the situation. See how strongly they feel about the matter. Be sure they have all of the facts. Let them know that their opinions are important to you.

- ⮑ Line up your allies. Who else is being drawn into this affair? Solicit their assistance.

- ⮑ Get another opinion from some trusted outsider. Perhaps he or she will have a different perspective on the matter.

- ⮑ Present your side of the story to your critics. Provide significant background information, including important but overlooked prior events that may help to explain current conditions. Be honest, factual, concerned and willing to accept whatever blame rightfully attaches to your company. Be sure to protect your credibility.

- ⮑ Accommodate the media. Try to develop a rapport with the reporters assigned to the story and encourage them to bring you information regarding the story for your comment. Be particularly attentive to those who fairly report your position on the issue rather than that of your attacker.

➲ Do not rely on the media to convey your message. Communicate directly with each of your customers and tell them what you can. Let them know that you want to stay in touch, and encourage them to call if they have questions or can provide you with any useful information.

➲ Repeat your story as often as necessary to be sure you're reaching all of the opinion-makers involved. Be consistent. Avoid speculation and reject hypothetical situations.

➲ Enhance your story whenever additional information becomes available or a new ally appears on the scene.

➲ If an unfavorable development forces you to modify your story, do so and explain why. You cannot be faulted for keeping an open mind and responding to new information.

11. Avoiding trouble with leases

PROBLEM: When you leased your current premises, you signed a "standard" lease with the owner. Now you have discovered that the lease contains a number of hidden conditions that may cause you a number of costly inconveniences.

DIAGNOSIS: Rather than the simple document that it often seems to be, a lease is a legal document and deserves careful examination *before* you sign it. The lease may not only include a lot of things that may be harmful, it may also omit a number of things that should be included.

PRESCRIPTION: If the lease is a substantial one, either in terms of the space involved, the cost of the lease or the length of the lease, it probably would be a good idea to have it reviewed by your attorney.

Regardless of who looks it over, however, a lease should address these considerations:

➲ How long will the lease run?
➲ How much is the rent?
➲ How much can your landlord increase the rent and under what circumstances?
➲ Can you renew the lease when it expires?
➲ Can you sublease some—or all—of your space?

➲ What services are included in the rent?
  • Electricity.
  • Heating, ventilation and air conditioning. (Commercial space rarely offers this service on a 24-hour basis. Holidays and weekends may not be covered either.)
  • Cleaning services. How thorough? How often?

➲ Who is responsible for insurance?

➲ Who pays for improvements?
  • Partitions.
  • Lighting.
  • Carpeting.
  • Painting.

➲ Who *owns* any added improvement? (Generally, if anything is firmly attached to the floor, wall or ceiling, it belongs to the landlord. Even window-mounted air conditioners may fall into this category.)

➲ Can competitors move into the building? Do you want a competitor next door or down the hall?

➲ What happens if the landlord goes broke? To be sure you're not thrown out on the street under such a situation, your lease should contain a standard "recognition" or nondisturbance clause.

12. Putting your agreements in writing

PROBLEM: At first, you were able to do business on the basis of a handshake. But now that the business has grown, it has become necessary to commit more and more things to writing. The question is: When is a letter no longer sufficient and when does it become necessary to negotiate a formal contract?

DIAGNOSIS: In many instances, a letter-contract or letter of agreement may be sufficient to cover the situation, but the more complex the transaction, the more important it is to enter into a contractual agreement. You are not only protecting yourself, but you are protecting your customers, partners or employees, as well, and they'll probably appreciate your consideration. This is business, after all, not a friendly little game of golf.

PRESCRIPTION: The process of preparing a contract helps to ensure that all of the details of the transaction have been worked out, that those details are accurate and complete, and that both you and your customer have been on the same wavelength during your discussions, *even if nobody ever consults the contract once it has been finalized.*

With so many American businesses downsizing these days, contracts become even more significant. The person with whom you negotiated your deal may not be around at a time some dispute arises.

Be on the alert anytime somebody tells you "We never enforce that clause" or "Don't worry about that paragraph." Negotiations should be concluded *before* a contract is drawn up, not afterward.

The more complex the agreement, the more important it is to have the contract reviewed by an attorney. Look for an attorney who is familiar with your size and type of business, and who has had experience in dealing with contracts similar to yours. And to cut costs, have the details of the contract worked out *before* you take it to the attorney.

A few situations for which a contract is necessary include:

- Partnership agreements, which should include details regarding capitalization, division of duties, how to calculate the business' profits, when to allow draws, how to value the business and (at times, the most important consideration) the procedure for buying someone out.
- Shareholders' agreements.
- Franchise agreements, including what the franchisor will provide in return for the franchise fee, the responsibilities of each party, any limitations on competing franchises and the circumstances under which the agreement may be terminated—by either party.
- Key employee contracts that govern the protection of trade secrets and prohibit certain types of competition, such as the use of customer/client lists or seeking employment with a competitor, if the employee ever leaves the company.
- Key supplier contracts that protect trade secrets and specify who is to provide what, by when, and at what cost.
- Warranties or guarantees that you may offer on your product/service.

Rule of thumb: It is worth drawing up a contract any time the cost of drawing one up *is less than the amount you stand to lose if your deal goes bad.*

13. Insuring yourself

PROBLEM: Like most small businesses, you cannot afford to take very many potentially costly risks. Proper insurance might help, but what kind do you need?

DIAGNOSIS: Wisely, you have recognized your vulnerability and are looking for sensible protection. Obviously, such protection also must be reasonably affordable.

PRESCRIPTION: To develop a comprehensive insurance plan, get the advice of a qualified insurance agent. Then check with another agent in order to get a second opinion. The second agent may think of something that the first agent overlooked.

Your business probably should be carrying at least four types of insurance:

- ⮑ Fire.
- ⮑ Liability.
- ⮑ Vehicle.
- ⮑ Workers' compensation.

It wouldn't be a bad idea to have your accountant and your lawyer look over your insurance package as well.

14. Avoiding high legal costs

PROBLEM: It seems like you have to see an attorney before you can do much of anything these days. The settlements being awarded by the courts are unbelievable, yet the cost of legal counsel isn't cheap either. How can you keep your legal expenses in line?

DIAGNOSIS: When you buy something from a supplier, you carefully investigate its quality and its price. You should take the same care when selecting an attorney.

PRESCRIPTION: The type of relationship you have with your attorney—and what you pay for his or her services—are subject to negotiation. Among the factors to consider are these:

- ⮑ Don't engage the first lawyer you meet; shop around. But once you have selected a lawyer, stay with him or her. Once your lawyer becomes familiar with your business, he or she will be much more capable of handling your legal affairs than some other lawyer, who would have to start over from scratch.

➲ Realize that the *cheapest* lawyer isn't necessarily the *best* lawyer to handle your business affairs.

➲ Discuss the matter of fees with your lawyer.

➲ Determine how you will be charged by your lawyer:
  • By the hour.
  • A flat fee.
  • A contingency fee.

➲ Ask your lawyer about ways to cut costs:
  • Will he or she accept an hourly fee instead of a contingency fee in some cases, if it were more economical for you?
  • Will your lawyer accept a lower hourly fee if you will guarantee him or her a certain amount of work throughout the year?

➲ Consult the lawyer on several matters at one time rather than making a separate trip every time some question comes up.

➲ Visit your lawyer during normal business hours rather than after-hours or on weekends.

➲ By reading the industry trade journals, belonging to trade associations and attending industry meetings, you can keep abreast of the important legal issues in your field, thereby giving you less reason to constantly ask questions of your lawyer.

➲ By sending your lawyer copies of trade journal articles and things of that nature, you can keep him or her informed about new developments in your field of business, thereby helping to reduce the amount of time that he or she will have to spend (and charge you for) doing research.

➲ Have the lawyer design forms for you to use in routine business transactions.

➲ Insist on an itemized statement each month.

➲ Ask for progress reports during prolonged cases.

➲ Find someone willing to share costs with you. If there are other parties involved in a lawsuit, for example, suggest sharing the legal expenses—but only if a conflict of interest is not involved.

➲ If your legal expenses are in excess of $30,000 a year or so, consider hiring an in-house legal counsel as an addition to your staff.

15. Taking deductions for a home office

PROBLEM: Rather than lease, furnish and staff an expensive office, you—and 39 million other American businesspeople—have opted to set up an office in your home. You know that some of your expenses are tax-deductible—but which ones?

DIAGNOSIS: You do not need to maintain an office in a separate room in order to qualify for a tax deduction. It is only necessary that you use separately identifiable space *exclusively* and *regularly* as your principal place of business or as a place where you meet with customers, patients or clients if that is a normal function of your business.

PRESCRIPTION: You must be able to convince the IRS that your in-home office is being used for the purpose of making a profit and not for the purpose of pursuing a hobby or avoiding taxes.

If you own your own home, you can depreciate that part of your house which is used as an office and you also can deduct a portion of your utilities. If, for example, one of the six rooms in your house is used as an office, deductible items can also include a portion of telephone expenses used for your business. If so, it is better to have a second line devoted exclusively to business purposes. The same would also be true for a dedicated fax line.

If you rent your home, you can deduct part of the rent as well as a comparable portion of your household utilities. If, for example, 10 percent of the floor space in your house is used for your business, you can deduct 10 percent of your rent, 10 percent of your home insurance, 10 percent of your heating and cooling expense, 10 percent of your electric bill and so on.

Even if your in-home office is used in the conduct of a *second* business, it may qualify for a tax deduction, but in order for *any* home office expense to be deductible, *each* business must qualify for the tax exemption. If *one* of the businesses fails to qualify, *none* of the office expense will be deductible.

To claim your home office deduction, complete Form 8829, "Expenses for Business Use of Your Home," and file it with your other income tax papers. If you are self-employed, expenses can be written off on Schedule C of your Form 1040. If you work for somebody else, your business expenses can be claimed as miscellaneous itemized deductions on Schedule A, with Form 2106 attached, subject to the 2 percent floor (you can only deduct any expenses which, when added to all other miscellaneous expenses, exceed 2 percent of your adjusted gross income).

To determine your special situation, see IRS Publication #587, "Business Use of Your Home," which includes criteria for using home deductions, limits, etc.

Note: Claiming an office in your home can be a handicap if you ever decide to sell the house. If you are eligible for a home office deduction during the year in which the house is sold, you may have to pay a tax on any gain that is attributable to the portion of the house that was used as an office.

16. Responding to change

PROBLEM: You attempt to stay on top of current trends and new technology, to explore every opportunity for growth and to see that your employees are always well-informed. Yet you're not growing. At times, it seems like all of your employees' hands are tied and their feet are set in cement.

DIAGNOSIS: The top job of every CEO is to listen and facilitate, not to talk and issue orders.

It has been said that there are two kinds of leaders: those who anticipate change and those who wait until the failure to change has created a crisis. Often, the leaders who fall into the latter category will fail.

PRESCRIPTION: American business sometimes spends a lot of time and effort on developing sports-related analogies and pursuing sports-related goals. Not to be outdone, we suggest that you can sidestep many potentially dangerous business situations if you *avoid*:

- ➲ Concentrating on "home runs." A big score is wonderful now and then, but day-in and day-out it's the "singles" that produce the best batting averages.

- ➲ Lacking flexibility. It is nice to have a good "switch hitter" available and to know that you can fall back on "Plan B" when you're in a pinch. To compete in today's high-energy market, companies must be adaptable.

- ➲ "Overcoaching." You must plan, but understand that nothing will happen until a decision is reached and a plan can be implemented. Don't overanalyze; *do something!*

- ➲ "Overcoaching II." Hustle and spirit generally will produce more results than a drawer full of plans.

⮑ Forgetting the value of "team spirit." It would be nice to be perfect, but one should never forget the role that such simple things as pride, joy, fun, excitement and just plain *play* contribute to the development of outstanding performance.

⮑ Too much "scouting." It is important to be on the lookout for new customers, but the best way to reach a new customer is through the word-of-mouth recommendation of an existing customer. Take care of the customers you have and the new customers will follow.

17. Medicine for business success

PROBLEM: You always labored under the belief that all there is to operating a business is to gather some capital, rent an office or storefront, hang out a sign and wait for the customers to come in.

Having done those things, you soon learned that operating a successful business involves a little bit more than that. Some of your acquaintances went bankrupt before they learned that lesson.

What are the elusive elements that separate the successful companies from the unsuccessful ones?

DIAGNOSIS: The high rate of bankruptcy among entrepreneurial companies testifies to the fact that too many owners simply did not learn and follow some very basic business practices.

PRESCRIPTION: Businesses fail as often from *not doing what is right* as they do from *doing things that are wrong*. These measures will provide the best odds for success.

⮑ Use the most appropriate tools available—computers, fax machines or whatever best suits the needs of your business.

⮑ Know who your best customers are and pamper them.

⮑ Involve your employees in the business. Let them help you solve problems and find better ways of handling things.

⮑ Constantly improve your communication—with employees, colleagues, customers and suppliers.

⮑ In promoting your business, stress the *benefits*, not the *features* of your product/service.

⮑ Develop a good relationship with your banker. Don't wait for some financial crisis to occur. Keep your banker updated regularly on how the company is doing.

➲ Learn to network. People tend to do business with people they know. Join local organizations and industry groups to broaden your contacts.

➲ Develop professional relationships ("strategic partnerships") with other small-business owners. Team up with them on projects that you can't handle alone. Refer business to each other. Help each other in emergencies or when the workload becomes too heavy.

➲ Survey your customers regularly to see how well you are satisfying their needs. Ask former customers why they left. Be prepared to make adjustments in your product or your method of doing business.

➲ Treat your employees well and provide them with the tools they need to do their work. Stay out of their way, be sensitive to their personal needs and reward good work.

➲ Hire professional help in such areas as accounting, law and obtaining governmental assistance.

➲ Look for a niche that is uniquely yours and concentrate on it. A competitor may be older, larger or better financed, but there are some things that you can do that they cannot— and that is your niche. Don't try to be all things to all people.

➲ Add value to your product/service by:
  • Giving something free with each purchase.
  • Developing a frequent-user program.
  • Offering a warranty or a money-back guarantee.
  • Customizing your work.

➲ When making major purchases, get several quotes before making your buy.

➲ Develop a variety of financial reports and learn to interpret them accurately. Such reports can tip you off to everything from embezzlement to the need for expansion.

Chapter 3

The bitter harvest of poor organization

18. Every project needs to be organized

PROBLEM: Your business has grown so fast that everyone is rushing to solve today's problems. Mistakes are repeated time after time. Nothing is consistent.

DIAGNOSIS: Your company seems to be suffering from two problems simultaneously: 1) Effective systems have not been established to see that your work gets done in the smoothest, most consistent and most profitable manner; and 2) your employees have not been instructed to follow the established procedures unless they have recommended a better one to management *and received management's approval to implement a change.*

PRESCRIPTION: Every company needs an up-to-date operations manual that spells out what is to be done and how to do it (see "Consistency counts: preparing your operations manual," in Chapter 1). Any time the procedures specified in the operations manual are not followed, the violator had better have a darned good reason.

Equally important are a set of management controls which 1) enable you and your key managers to tell how well the company is doing in terms of following your business plan, and 2) alert you whenever there is the need to make adjustments to that plan.

Go over your business plan, asking yourself: "What has to happen before something else can happen?" Based on that review, set up control points to keep everything moving smoothly and to assure that no bottlenecks develop along the way.

➲ Devise ways of *showing* how well your plan is progressing according to:
- A time line.
- A calendar.
- Some computer software that is specifically designed for project planning.

➲ Assign a schedule for completion of every task.

➲ Designate someone to make sure that every critical function is being done, and done right.

➲ Recognize your constraints:
- What are your limitations?
- What resources do you have to work with?
  1. Money.
  2. Manpower.
  3. Equipment.
  4. Time.

- What problems are you likely to encounter?
  1. Competition.
  2. Changing market conditions.
  3. Increasing costs.

➲ Keep track of the results:
- Determine the day-to-day operational things you will review daily or weekly.
- Determine the "big events" you will review monthly.
- Outline how you want your business to develop and grow over the next three to five years and check to see how well you're doing in reaching those objectives every six months or so.

➲ If the worst should occur and your plan doesn't work, what can you do?
- Develop a fall-back plan.

19. Your employees: assets or liabilities?

PROBLEM: You've become so frustrated with the personnel problems plaguing your company that you often wish you could automate everything and eliminate all of your employees.

DIAGNOSIS: Boy, do you have an attitude! Or maybe you simply prefer to blame your own inadequacies on those who work for you.

Viewing your employees as an expense, rather than as an asset is an attitude to avoid in business. The next time you write an employee's paycheck, ask yourself how much that person has contributed to the company. The answer may surprise you.

PRESCRIPTION: If you are plagued by problems, you may be guilty of violating one of the five other major organizational sins:

➲ Hiring down, rather than up. Always try to employ the most talented people you can find.

➲ Hiring talented people, but not letting them exercise their talents. Do not impose inflexible rules upon your employees. It is to your advantage to bring out the best in all of them.

➲ Making do with the people you have, rather than hiring the people you need. By the time some businesses have been around awhile, they consist of a genuine hodgepodge of people. This is because the company has hired a variety of people to fill the needs of an opportunity over the years, rather than the needs of the company's strategic direction (as spelled out in the company's business plan). Once the opportunity goes away, the people remain, and soon the driving force within the company shifts from meeting the needs of the market to seeing that its people are kept employed.

➲ Losing your clarity of purpose. A successful company needs a good organizational infrastructure, coupled with a clear sense of purpose. That purpose needs to be communicated throughout the company, along with clear mission statements, written policies and procedures, job descriptions that describe everyone's responsibilities and accountabilities, and understandable organizational charts.

➲ Creating an organizational hierarchy that puts the preservation of the organization ahead of service to the customers.

20. Whom do you trust?

PROBLEM: To operate a business of any size, it is necessary to create an organization. One person simply cannot handle everything.

Realizing that organizations cannot be built overnight, what steps are necessary to build a strong, effective organizational infrastructure?

DIAGNOSIS: Focus on the *quality* of your people. Determine which ones are your star performers.

PRESCRIPTION: By raising your standards relentlessly, you can begin to identify and groom talent at every level, as well as rid yourself of any deadwood. A demanding standard, accompanied by some inevitable firings, does not demoralize the other workers. They would rather be held to a high standard—and work with those who feel the same way. It is far more demoralizing to them to see mediocrity tolerated and rewarded.

Set out a one-year game plan:

- ⊃ Choose candidates whose odds of success are high based on past performance.
- ⊃ Set goals for each key employee and department. Focus on a few high-impact results. Watch to see what's working and where improvements can be made.
- ⊃ Give key employees challenging, fresh, taxing assignments.
- ⊃ Make sure talented people don't stay in one job too long.
- ⊃ Make reassignment decisions once a year as part of an annual performance review.
- ⊃ If it appears that an assignment is not working out, try to find some other slot for that individual.
- ⊃ Don't be afraid to hire outsiders at high levels if in-house candidates are lacking.
- ⊃ Be sure the best achievers are rewarded appropriately.

21. Are your records reliable?

PROBLEM: You have maintained your own records since you first went into business, but now you realize that accurate and thorough record-keeping is going to take a great deal more time and effort than you have been devoting to it.

DIAGNOSIS: Many people dislike the task of dealing with paperwork, but accurate, up-to-date records are essential to a successful business, as you have learned.

Determine what records are needed, who will maintain them, which format is most efficient and how often they should be reviewed.

Remember, too, that too much paperwork can be just as wasteful as too little.

PRESCRIPTION: Bookkeeping can be handled from inside or outside the business office. Your accountant, lawyer or banker can help you determine your needs for an inside bookkeeper or an outside accounting service.

A good system should include:

- ➲ A system for the accurate and timely recording of your company's:
  - Cash receipts.
  - Disbursements.
  - Sales.
  - Operating expenses.
- ➲ Periodic statements, including:
  - Balance sheet (a statement of assets and liabilities as of a specified date).
  - Income statement (results of operations for a given period of time).
  - A statement of changes in your financial position.
  - Records of accounts receivable.
  - Records of payments due.
- ➲ State and federal income tax returns.
- ➲ Social Security tax returns.
- ➲ Employee tax withholding records.
- ➲ Property tax records.
- ➲ Other tax-related documents.

22. What records should you keep?

PROBLEM: After years of doing business, the amount of records you have retained has grown to mountainous proportions. Can you dispose of some of them?

DIAGNOSIS: Records retention is almost a science of its own, but finding a particular document once it has been stored away is equally important. Increasingly, the latter calls for the skill of a Sherlock Holmes.

PRESCRIPTION: Consult your accountant and your attorney to determine what records you must retain and for how long. Tax records, for example, should be maintained for a specific period of time.

Also determine who is to be responsible for disposing of old records and the manner in which it is to be done.

Today, most banks offer a system that makes it unnecessary for you to save your old checks. Many companies are using microfilm or microfiche, rather than storing old documents in filing cabinets or boxes in the basement. And of course, the increasing use of computers enables many companies to store away vital records electronically.

23. What computers can (and can't) do

PROBLEM: Your accounting problems have simply gotten out of hand. They take too long, they're prone to mistakes and your files are growing faster than your business.

DIAGNOSIS: You sound like a prime candidate for computerization. If you don't understand them, hire someone who does. Properly used, they're worth the trouble and the expense.

PRESCRIPTION: Computers are excellent tools for many things. For a small business, computers are best adapted to such applications as:

- Accounts receivable.
- Accounts payable.
- Order entry.
- Inventory control.
- General ledger.

Approach computerization slowly and carefully. Computerize one application at a time. When it is running smoothly, move on to the next. Always remember that computers have their weaknesses, as well as their strengths. For example, they are *not* suitable for:

- Solving broad, poorly defined problems.
- Cleaning up errors in your manual systems.
- Forecasting or doing trend analyses until you have had several years of experience and collected a great deal of historical data with which they can work.
- Solving problems that require subjective evaluations.
- Solving all of your production scheduling problems.
- Saving money by eliminating human employees.

Remember, too, that computers *aren't always right*. You need to build in certain checks and balances to be sure you get what you expect to get from a computer.

24. When you must decide—*now*

PROBLEM: For whatever reason, you have a hard time making decisions. You procrastinate and equivocate, but you find it very difficult to state a cut-and-dried decision, especially when pressed to do so.

DIAGNOSIS: The ability to make decisions is critical to problem-solving—and problem-solving is essential to operating any business.

PRESCRIPTION: Practicing the following steps should help you to make decisions in a more timely manner:

- ⮑ Define the problem. State your primary and secondary aims. Examine the things to be accomplished in broad, general terms.

- ⮑ Redefine the problem in more specific terms. Translate your general aims into quantitative goals, interspersing sub-goals among the main goals. Specify times, dollars and units.

- ⮑ See how the new goals fit in with the overall organizational goals. Don't give high priority to anything that doesn't conform to the goals of your basic business plan.

- ⮑ Line up alternatives. Judge them against your instinctive choice. Consider each alternate objectively. Look for the foreseeable consequences of each.

- ⮑ Review your resources. How much time, manpower and money are available to support your decision?

- ⮑ List and evaluate the consequences if you should decide incorrectly. Also consider the consequences of doing nothing at all.

- ⮑ Sell the decision. Talk with key people for their reaction to your idea, and try to draw out their objections and obstacles to your decision.

- ⮑ Make the decision and implement it. By word and action, make sure everyone is aware of your continuing commitment to the plan you have adopted.

25. Putting time on your side

PROBLEM: Increasingly, you notice that your employees are having a hard time getting their work done. They simply don't seem capable of using their time effectively. What can you do to help?

DIAGNOSIS: You can help them to fight procrastination by finding out what types of work they prefer to put off. Knowing that, you may be able to assign your work differently, giving each person the kind of work he most enjoys doing.

PRESCRIPTION: Other means of improving your performance within a limited period of time include:

- ⮑ Encouraging your employees to prepare written to-do lists. (Don't include such routine tasks as answering the phone and opening the mail.)
- ⮑ Having them prioritize their lists.

If the employees will do these two simple things each day, they will have no excuse for not getting to work as soon as they reach work in the morning. Every time they scratch off an item on their lists, they will benefit from a sense of accomplishment for having completed that portion of their work.

26. How to avoid mixed signals

PROBLEM: You have encountered countless situations in which a key employee has contended that you told him or her one thing, while you have insisted that you said something else. How do you resolve such disputes?

DIAGNOSIS: This is so simple, it probably doesn't deserve a response in this book—but it's such a common problem, it's obvious that many small businessmen still haven't heard the message.

PRESCRIPTION: *Put your instructions in writing!*
There are a number of other reasons for making sure various types of messages are committed to writing:

- ⮑ To refresh your memory.
- ⮑ To remind you of a commitment.
- ⮑ To give you time to reread, absorb, consider and appraise facts or ideas expressed in the written message.
- ⮑ To document events and guidelines for future planning.
- ⮑ To assure accuracy.
- ⮑ To prepare reports.
- ⮑ To clarify thinking.
- ⮑ To save time.
- ⮑ To organize.
- ⮑ To keep lists of facts, addresses, dates, figures, etc.
- ⮑ To keep track of what has been read or said.

27. Reorganizing before you must

PROBLEM: Sales are down, manufacturing costs are up, distribution problems have arisen and there is a rash of unrest among the employees. Could there be a common cause?

DIAGNOSIS: At first blush, it would appear that your company has reached the point where some serious reorganization is required.

PRESCRIPTION: Organization development is the ongoing process of devising self-improving and self-correcting means by which the organization will change and improve. It involves:

- Confronting the problems that slow down the organization.
- Getting decisions made at the level where the facts are.
- Developing effective teamwork.
- Dealing with conflicts openly and constructively.
- Increasing awareness of how *process* affects *performance*.

The process of organization development involves:

- Identifying able people.
- Testing them under fire.
- Providing chances for decision-making under increasingly difficult situations.
- Allowing managers to increase their span of control.
- Helping managers develop confidence.
- Basing judgment of potential on performance.
- Rewarding those who are accountable and take risks.
- Providing opportunity for upward mobility.
- Encouraging responsibility at the lowest possible level.

Chapter 4

Getting the money you need

28. Keeping enough cash on hand

PROBLEM: On paper, your business is doing just fine. But there never seems to be enough cash to handle day-to-day matters.

DIAGNOSIS: Without cash, you're bankrupt. Your business may be showing a paper profit, but if you can't handle your daily bills, you're at the mercy of your creditors.

PRESCRIPTION: While you are making more long-range adjustments to your cash position, you need to generate cash any way you can, such as:
- Spread out your accounts payable.
- Speed up your accounts receivable.
- Factor your accounts receivable, that is, sell the accounts receivable at a discounted price.
- Create an imaginative marketing program designed to generate immediate cash.

29. When you need to borrow

PROBLEM: A sudden increase in sales has thrown your entire business into a state of flux. Your accounts receivable are way up, your inventory is way down, the cost of goods sold has changed and you're having a cash crunch—all at the same time.

DIAGNOSIS: When your sales picture changes unexpectedly, the repercussions generally are felt throughout the company. Most often, it becomes necessary to borrow some money to help you handle your immediate needs as you bring your other problems into balance.

PRESCRIPTION: Ideally, you will recognize the need for more money before you encounter a cash-flow crisis.

Try to determine:

- ➲ How much do you expect sales to increase?
- ➲ Will the cost of goods sold increase accordingly?
- ➲ How will these events effect your operating expenses?

The answers to these questions will let you determine whether the increase in sales also will produce an increase in your net profit.

Also, take into account the effect of uncontrollable factors that are occurring outside the company:

- ➲ The general economy: A change in the interest rate can affect your return on investment greatly.
- ➲ The economic health of your industry.
- ➲ What your competition is doing.

To determine how much money you may need, calculate your rate of growth. To calculate this figure, divide the year's sales increase by last year's annual sales. Applying this ratio to your associated expenses will show you how much capital you are likely to need and, hence, whether it would be appropriate to secure a bank loan.

30. Unusual loan sources

PROBLEM: You have determined that you need to borrow some money for business operations. Other than your local bank, what borrowing options do you have?

DIAGNOSIS: Always shop around before you negotiate a loan. Rates and conditions vary almost daily, and you want to find the most favorable terms available at the time you arrange for the loan.

PRESCRIPTION: A relatively new kind of loan is now available, and many businesspeople are not yet aware of it. It is a "microloan," backed by the Small Business Administration.

Designed to provide business funding for groups that traditionally have had trouble obtaining conventional loans, such as home-based businesses, part-time businesses, low-income individuals and firms owned by women or minorities, these loans carry a limit of $25,000, even though the average is about $10,000.

A microloan, which can be used for working capital, inventory, supplies, furniture, fixtures, machinery and equipment, is approved locally by one of 96 nonprofit groups appointed by the SBA to administer the program.

For more details on a microloan, contact your local SBA office or call 1-800-827-5722.

If such a loan does not suit your needs, you could send $1.50 to obtain a copy of *Steps to Small Business Financing* from the American Bankers Association, Customer Service Center, P.O. Box 630544, Baltimore, MD 21263-0544.

It also might be worth the $10 cost to get a list of the 300 members of the National Association of Small Business Investment Companies who have SBA funds available. Write to the association at 1199 North Fairfax St., #200, Alexandria, VA 22314, or phone 703-683-1601.

Other sources of help when seeking funding:

- Nashville Minority Business Development Center, Nashville, Tennessee.
- Black Business Association, Los Angeles, California.
- Rebuild L.A., Los Angeles, California.
- Center for Small Business Studies, Washington, D.C.

31. Which loan is best for you?

PROBLEM: Which manner of borrowing money is most beneficial to someone in your circumstances?

DIAGNOSIS: Determine exactly how much money you need, for how long and how much you can afford to pay for it.

PRESCRIPTION: A small company usually seeks short-term financing for an emergency, to finance its receivables or its inventory, or to take advantage of an inventory bargain. Technically, "short-term" means a loan that runs for one year or less.

Short-term loans generally involve:

Lines of credit

- A specific sum earmarked for your company to draw on, as needed, over a predetermined period. Interest is charged only on the amount actually withdrawn. A commitment fee ranging from one-half to 1 percent usually is imposed, although some banks will waive the fee if the company maintains a certain amount in its account during the loan period.

- A *nonbinding* line of credit, the least expensive form, offers no guarantees. If your financial position deteriorates, your credit will be curtailed.
- A *committed* line of credit, which may entail paying a fee of about 2 percent, assures you that the funds will be there when you need them.
- A *revolving* line of credit requires an annual review and renewal. Similar to a revolving charge account, a revolving line accrues interest only on the funds actually borrowed, and there are generally no other costs involved.

Loans on inventory

- The collateral for the loan is the inventory itself.
- Funds can be borrowed, as needed, and repaid in installments as the inventory is sold and the receivables are collected.
- Involve an annual "clean up," which means the account must be fully paid up at least 30 days out of the year.

Commercial loans

- The loan typically is repaid in a lump sum at the end of the term, which usually runs from three to six months.

Accounts receivable financing

- Accounts generally must be less than 60 days past due and the customers themselves must be creditworthy.
- Banks typically will advance 65 to 80 percent of the receivables' face value.
- Generally, incoming checks are passed on to the bank, which will take its portion and then deposit the rest to your account, charging interest only on the amount still outstanding.
- Most banks will set a minimum on such financing, based on the cost of monitoring such loans.

Factoring

- A bank or factoring company buys your receivables outright at a discount.
- Generally, such a sale takes you out of the loop since the bank assumes all of the credit risk and takes on all collection responsibilities.

➲ *Non-notification factoring* means that you continue to collect the payments and forward them to the new owner, which keeps your customer from knowing that you are using a factoring company.

Medium-term loans, generally running from one to five years in length, are typically used to finance the purchase of machinery and equipment, plant alterations and expansion. Such loans usually involve:

Term loan

➲ Such loans frequently provide 80 to 90 percent of the necessary financing and include a refinancing clause, allowing the loan to be renewed, if necessary.

➲ They typically call for quarterly payments, including principal and interest.

Monthly payment business loan

➲ Payments, either monthly or quarterly, include principal and interest.

Long-term loans are those that extend beyond five years and are the most difficult to get. Usually, they are used to purchase real estate, finance a major expansion or acquisition, or finance a startup. Such loans can include:

Commercial and industrial mortgage

➲ Most banks will approve a mortgage up to 75 percent of the property's appraised value.

➲ Although 25-year mortgages are sometimes available, five- or 10-year loans with a final "balloon" payment are more common. When the final payment comes due, the loan is refinanced.

Real estate loan

➲ Available to those who already own real estate and want to borrow against it.

➲ A *wrap-around mortgage* differs from a second mortgage in that the bank tightens its control by receiving all of your mortgage payments and then relaying the payment to the holder of the first mortgage.

➲ If mortgaged property has appreciated substantially, consider refinancing, but you will have to give up the old interest rate and take on a new, perhaps higher rate.

Personal loan

➲ Usually easier to negotiate than a business loan.

➲ An individual guarantees your loan with property such as real estate, securities, savings passbooks or certificates of deposit.

Asset-based loan

➲ The type of loan generally used to finance a leveraged buyout, the company's own assets provide the security for the loan. Such assets include real estate, machinery, inventory, raw materials, receivables—almost anything of value.

➲ May provide up to 70 percent of the acquisition cost, but you will be charged the bank's prime rate plus 2 or 3 percent.

32. Acquiring a letter of credit

PROBLEM: As a backup for the business, you feel it might be helpful to establish a letter of credit.

DIAGNOSIS: Although letters of credit can serve a purpose, you can achieve the same purpose by increasing the net worth of your company.

PRESCRIPTION: All letters of credit are secured by something of value, which can include:

➲ Real estate.

➲ Machinery.

➲ Equipment.

➲ Inventory.

➲ Stocks and bonds.

➲ Bank deposits.

➲ Accounts receivable.

➲ Signed, irrevocable contracts.

- The personal signature of a company principal (although this places the individual's personal assets in jeopardy).
- The "guarantee" of a close business associate, such as a customer, a supplier or a company under the same ownership as yours.

33. Some surprising government aids

PROBLEM: You need some additional operating capital for your business.

DIAGNOSIS: Funds are available through some rather unexpected agencies of the federal government.

PRESCRIPTION: Many people are aware of the Small Business Administration and the sources of funding made available through it. What many people do *not* know is that a number of other government agencies also have funds available to help small businesses.

- The Department of Agriculture offers National Wool Act Payments to encourage the domestic production of wool.
- The Department of Commerce has money for fisheries development and "utilization" research (new product development).
- All federal agencies and any company that has a contract with the federal government amounting to $500,000 or more in services or $1 million or more for construction *must* spend 20 percent of that contract on hiring small business subcontractors and 5 percent of the contract on hiring minority-owned subcontractors. The 5 percent earmarked for minority-owned businesses is *in addition to* the 20 percent that must go to small businesses.

For information about federal aid programs, refer to the *Catalog of Federal Domestic Assistance*, published by the U.S. Government Printing Office. For information about both state and federal aid, refer to *Government Giveaways for Entrepreneurs*, by Matthew Lesko, Information USA, 1992.

34. Personal sources of funding

PROBLEM: You need some funding, but have been having problems obtaining it due to a recessionary economy.

DIAGNOSIS: Consider the sources of funding that may be close at hand and require no lengthy approval process.

PRESCRIPTION: You have your own resources that can be converted to cash, and your family and friends can provide additional funding, when necessary.

Your own resources include:

➲ Home:
- A second mortgage.
- A home-equity loan (one of the few remaining forms of interest that is still income-tax deductible).

➲ Insurance:
- A loan against the cash value of your life insurance policy usually carries a low interest rate.

➲ Credit union.

➲ Retirement plan:
- Sometimes it is possible to withdraw money from a retirement plan, but you will have to pay taxes on the amount you withdraw plus a 10 percent penalty if you take the money out before you reach the age of 59½.

➲ Credit cards:
- May be okay for small amounts, but remember that the interest rates usually are very high.

A family "gift" can be beneficial to you and the giver *if you obey certain tax regulations*. Anybody can give any number of individuals up to $10,000 a year each *without incurring the federal gift tax* (which applies to the giver, not the recipient). This means that a mother can give $10,000 to her daughter and $10,000 to her son-in-law, and the father can do the same, thereby transferring $40,000 *in one year* from the older couple to the younger couple. The younger couple receives the money they need for their business, and the older couple removes $40,000 from the value of their taxable estate.

35. Using your vendors as partners

PROBLEM: You feel that you could improve your cash flow if you could persuade your vendors to lower their prices.

DIAGNOSIS: Don't forget that your vendors have businesses to run, too. Talk to your vendors about some unorthodox financing options that might tempt them to lower their prices.

PRESCRIPTION: There are a couple of financing methods that might induce your vendors to lower their prices for you, or to help you improve your cash flow:

Fixed price. By buying the vendor's product outright and paying for it immediately, you may be able to negotiate a lower price. There is no risk to the vendor, who receives the money immediately, thereby improving cash flow. In exchange, he or she may very well be willing to lower the price, producing a savings for you.

Incentives. If you need to improve your cash flow, it might be worthwhile to pay your vendors a little bit *more* for their goods—*if* the vendor will wait until you have completed your sale and received payment for it. Such an arrangement costs you a little more, but it improves your cash flow, while the vendor gains some extra profit in exchange for delaying receipt of his money.

36. Improving the way you handle credit

PROBLEM: True, the economy could be better, but it seems like you're having an uncommon number of credit problems with your customers.

DIAGNOSIS: A businessperson is wise to manage the receivables in a prudent, yet flexible, manner regardless of the state of the economy.

PRESCRIPTION: Analyze your company's credit and collection procedures to determine:

➲ Who is responsible for calling delinquent accounts?
- Don't be afraid you'll lose a customer by calling to ask for money. Most companies want to pay their bills.
- If the first call, probably fielded by a clerk or bookkeeper, does not produce results, ask for the president of the company on the next call.

➲ When should the first call be made?
- As soon as the bill becomes overdue. In a tough economy, a troubled account can be out of business within 60 or 90 days.
- The first call sends the message that you pay close attention to business.

➲ What should be said during that first call?

- Ask for your money in a friendly, but firm tone.
- Instead of seeming combative, show that you are willing to negotiate a mutually satisfactory solution to the problem.
- Ask when you can expect payment, and for what amount.
- Be sure to get the name of the person you are talking to.

If the check doesn't arrive on the day specified, call back. Don't wait more than another day or two. Speak to the same person and ask if the check went out. If the account remains unpaid:

➲ Review the customer's record to see if you want to retain him or her as a customer.

➲ If you do, formulate the terms of your final offer for payment and see that they are sent to the president of the company personally.

➲ If you determine that the customer is not all that important, don't hesitate: Turn the matter over to a collection agency.

On an ongoing basis, you can help to prevent slow-pay problems by:

➲ Running credit checks on your biggest customers at least once a year. Do the same whenever a new customer places a large order.

➲ Asking trade associations for information pertinent to the financial health of your customer.

➲ Watch the trade publications for information—good and bad—about your customers.

➲ Watch for early signs of trouble:
- Slow payments.
- Small, partial payments.
- Frequent changes from one bank to another.

➲ Involve your sales force:
- Have them watch for signs of trouble, such as layoffs or other types of cutbacks.
- Have them listen for signs of trouble when talking to their contacts within the company.
- Have them listen for signs of trouble when they are socializing with their competitors or with their customers' competitors.

37. Speeding up collections

PROBLEM: When your customers are slow making payment, the results ripple throughout your company.

DIAGNOSIS: Be tactful, by all means, but discuss your problems candidly with your customers.

PRESCRIPTION: Some things that will help you to maintain your perspective while you are working to solve your problems with slow-pays:

- Determine how many concessions you can make.
- Consider how reliable your customer is.
- Put your cards on the table and express your concerns candidly.
- Look for a compatible solution that will not hurt your business.
- If the customer owes a large amount, make a personal visit to discuss the matter. It the amount is small, a phone call will do.
- If you are dealing with an old, reliable customer who is having a temporary setback, consider making what is owed an outstanding bill (due in, say, 60 days), then revising the terms for any new purchases (from, say, payment in 45 days to payment in 30 days).
- Another possible strategy: If the customer will place a larger order than usual, allow him or her 60 days in which to make payment rather than 30 days.
- If the customer is in an uncertain, risky position, ask for C.O.D. payment for all new purchases. Once his or her financial position improves, negotiate more convenient terms for payment.

38. If you have to go to court...

PROBLEM: After repeatedly trying to collect from a customer, you have determined that it will be necessary to take the customer to Small Claims Court.

DIAGNOSIS: The maximum amount you can sue for in a Small Claims Court varies from state to state, but this is an excellent way to collect small sums ignored by contentious customers.

PRESCRIPTION: Generally speaking, taking a customer to Small Claims Court does not necessitate hiring an attorney. Indeed, some states specifically bar attorneys from Small Claims Court.

Pursuing this course of action will take a little time, and probably will entail the payment of a modest filing fee.

Small claims means precisely that; in some states, the maximum amount you can claim in Small Claims Court is just $1,000. In other states, the ceiling is higher.

If the customer owes you a sum greater than you can claim through action in Small Claims Court, you will have to file suit in a higher court.

Chapter 5

Do you have the right people?

39. Selecting new employees

PROBLEM: Your employees don't seem to be of the caliber that you need to run your business effectively. They are either incapable, uncommunicative, hard to lead or otherwise disruptive to the company's work flow.

DIAGNOSIS: This is the kind of problem that could go either of two ways: 1) Either you and/or your senior staff are not doing your part to draw the best effort from your employees; or 2) your employee selection process needs some rethinking.

PRESCRIPTION: Assuming that the problem is in the way you screen, select and hire your employees, examine the following as possible ways to improve the process:

- ➲ Prepare yourself for the interview by familiarizing yourself with the candidate's resume in advance.
- ➲ Before the interview takes place, prepare a list of questions to ask the candidate.
- ➲ Know what you are selecting a person to do.
- ➲ Ask the candidate open-ended questions.
- ➲ Allow the candidate to do most of the talking.
- ➲ Keep the interview flowing by using such questions and statements as:
  - • Why?
  - • Then what did you do?
  - • Tell me some more about that.

➲ Give your full attention to the candidate. Take only essential notes to help you remember such things as names, dates and statistics.

➲ Focus on the interview. Do not let the conversation drift to mutual acquaintances, common experiences, travels, hobbies or other interesting but unimportant factors.

➲ Watch for signs of maturity and accountability. Does the candidate accept responsibility for his or her decisions, achievements and mistakes? How objective is he or she?

➲ Ask such questions as:
  • Why did you leave (or are you thinking of leaving) your last job?
  • What did you like best about your last job?
  • If you could have made any improvements on your last job, what would they have been? Why?
  • What was your most interesting assignment?
  • Who was the best person you ever worked for, worked with or had working for you, and why?
  • What types of people annoy you the most?
  • What would you like to be doing five years from now?
  • What is most important to you: the money or the type of work you will be doing?
  • How would you describe yourself?
  • What motivates you to put forth your best effort?
  • If you were hiring a person for this position, what qualities would you be looking for?

➲ Watch out for braggarts.

➲ Check the candidate's references carefully.

➲ Don't make spot decisions.

➲ Weigh the candidate's potential in three broad categories:
  • Job aptitude.
  • Work attitude.
  • Ability to fit in with colleagues.

40. How to pick winners

PROBLEM: Your company is in an out-of-the-way location, making it difficult at times to attract new people from jobs in larger markets or more attractive regions.

DIAGNOSIS: You have to make your job offer sound more attractive than someone else's. Put yourself in the job candidate's shoes and position yourself to sell the benefits of the job.

PRESCRIPTION: Don't try to handle the task by yourself. Let other key members of your organization help out. For example: If the candidate is a woman, let some of your key female employees talk to her. If the candidate is a person in his or her mid-30s, have some of your same-age employees involved in the interview.

When interviewing a job candidate, first weed out the most unlikely prospects yourself and then let others in the company interview the candidates that remain.

See if there are other considerations to take into account before the candidate can reach a decision to relocate for your job.

- ⊃ The spouse must also find a new job.
- ⊃ The children will have to change schools.
- ⊃ Husband or wife is reluctant to move away from family, friends or the environment in which they have lived for a long time.
- ⊃ The candidate will have difficulty finding a new house or selling the old one.
- ⊃ Is the candidate under pressure to accept another offer?

Position yourself to act as the candidate's advocate during the employment negotiations.

Since job candidates are most fearful of things that are unknown, give them as much information as possible about the company, their key co-workers, the town and so on. Have other employees talk to them about the change.

41. Why hire a senior citizen?

PROBLEM: Suddenly, there has been a lot of local pressure to offer jobs to the community's senior citizens. Is that better than hiring young people who may be easier to train and who ought to stay around longer?

DIAGNOSIS: More and more, seniors who are still in good health but may have been "downsized," replaced or retired are returning to the work force for a number of reasons—need for income, bored, want to do something meaningful. Many employers have the opportunity to take advantage of their wisdom and experience.

PRESCRIPTION: Obviously, the type of the business and the difficulty of the work under consideration have a great deal to do with the advisability of employing a senior citizen. But, generally, there are a number of reasons for doing so:

⊃ **Customer service**

- Older people tend to remain calmer and more courteous when dealing with an upset customer.
- In many fields, seniors have had more life experiences that will enable them to respond to a customer's needs.
- Many customers find seniors less "threatening" than a younger worker.

⊃ **Reliability**

- Seniors are less prone to unwarranted absenteeism.
- Seniors are more likely to check their facts, rather than to shoot from the hip when asked for advice.
- Seniors are more likely to admit to an error, rather than lie, pass the buck or make excuses.

⊃ **Loyalty**

- You are less likely to have high turnover among older employees.

42. When family is involved

PROBLEM: What if your business involves numerous members of your immediate family, both as investors and as employees? Too often, business differences become *family* differences, leading to inter- and intra-family bickering. Can these things be avoided?

DIAGNOSIS: An old saying cautions that "an ounce of prevention is worth a pound of cure." Problems in family businesses really are no different than problems in nonfamily businesses except when the participants let personalities rule over good business judgment.

Before trouble arises, take the time to set up some devices that will enable members of the family to voice their concerns, but without disrupting the operation of the business.

PRESCRIPTION: When you consider adding a family member to the firm as an employee:

⊃ Deal objectively with their qualifications.

⊃ Consider having a young person gain some experience elsewhere before joining the family business.

When a family member is employed by the business:

➲ Be sure the individual's area(s) of responsibility are clearly defined.

➲ Define the roles of other family members who are working in the business.

➲ Divide the business responsibilities according to each person's particular area of expertise.

➲ If the individual is to be effective, be sure he or she has the latitude to do his or her work effectively.

➲ Be sure the working hours are clearly understood in advance, as well as the salary, vacation policies and other perks.

➲ Clearly define who reports to whom.

➲ Delegate office space and equipment thoughtfully so as not to favor one employee over another.

➲ If a difference arises, be sure it involves an issue, not an emotion.

If the family member is involved in the business financially or legally, but not involved in the running of the business:

➲ Work together on estate planning.

➲ Establish a family council to resolve any problems not directly related to the operation of the business.

43. Minimum wage exemptions

PROBLEM: You've wanted to hire individuals whose physical or mental handicaps don't allow them to do the job as effectively as someone else, but can't afford to pay a full wage. The sad fact is, such employees have not proved as productive as other employees that you can hire even at the legal minimum wage.

DIAGNOSIS: There is a provision in the Fair Labor Standards Act that can be helpful to you in providing work for the disadvantaged.

PRESCRIPTION: The FLSA stipulates that individuals "...whose earning or productive capacity is impaired by a physical or mental disability, including those related to age or injury, for the work to be performed" may be exempted from the minimum wage requirement.

For further information on exceptions to minimum wage, contact the Office of Program Operations, Wage and Hour Division, Employment Standards Administration, U.S. Department of Labor, Room S-3028, 200 Constitution Ave. NW, Washington, DC 20210, phone (202) 219-8353.

Chapter 6

Managing employees

44. No train, no gain

PROBLEM: Having come from diverse backgrounds, your employees approach their work from different angles, some good and some not as good. You wish there were more uniformity, both in their performance and work ethic.

DIAGNOSIS: Such uniformity results from on-the-job training and experience. Waiting for experience to bring about a change is more uncertain and it certainly takes longer. A good training program should do the job.

PRESCRIPTION: On-the-job training involves more than "fact-stuffing." It involves teaching the employee what you do, why you do it, why you do it *the way* you do, what your values are, how you expect your clients to be treated, how you deal with your suppliers, what you expect of an employee, how you try to treat your employees, and much more. Your purpose is to convert an "outsider" into a trusted and valuable "partner" in your business operation.

Knowing that he or she is competent and doing a good job builds self-confidence and improves the morale of an employee.

Among the things that ought to be included in an employee training program:

- ➲ Your company's policies and procedures.
- ➲ How to listen and communicate.
- ➲ How to resolve conflicts.
- ➲ Time management.
- ➲ The importance of productivity, efficiency and quality.
- ➲ The importance of simplifying processes and reducing waste.
- ➲ How to conduct focused meetings.
- ➲ The latest advances in technology.

One company certifies its employees after they have completed the in-house training program. Once certified, employees receive a 20-percent increase in their hourly wages.

At Corning, employees are expected to spend 5 percent of their working time on training. Other company employees, *not* professional educators, conduct most of their training classes.

At Federal Express, workers take computer-based job competency tests every six to 12 months. If an employee gets a low score on the tests, it leads to remedial action.

45. Overtime pay during training?

PROBLEM: Your company may employ a lot of part-time and minimum-wage personnel. For their own self-improvement as well as to enhance their performance on the job, you have created a mandatory training program that is conducted for the employees after-hours. Some of the employees feel that they should receive overtime pay for attending these classes.

DIAGNOSIS: It would appear that the payment of overtime would be exempted under a provision in the Fair Labor Standards Act.

PRESCRIPTION: The FLSA states: "...employees who lack a high school diploma or who have not completed the eighth grade may be required by their employer to spend up to 10 hours a workweek in remedial reading or training in other basic skills that are not job-specific, as long as they are paid their normal wages for the hours spent in training. *Such employees need not be paid overtime premium pay for their training hours.*"

To be absolutely sure that your situation is covered under this provision, contact the Office of Program Operations, Wage and Hour Division, Employment Standards Administration, U.S. Department of Labor, Room S-3028, 200 Constitution Ave. NW, Washington, DC 20210, phone (202) 219-8353.

46. Too much work—too few people

PROBLEM: You have too much business, but too little capital to hire the help you need.

DIAGNOSIS: Until you reach a stronger financial position, look for some creative ways to get the help you need without committing to all the costs involved in hiring a full-time employee.

PRESCRIPTION: There are a number of alternatives to full-time help you can investigate when you need some added staffing:

- ➲ Hire part-time employees.
- ➲ Work with temporary-help agencies.
- ➲ Provide incentives (overtime pay, etc.) to encourage greater productivity from your present employees.
- ➲ Contract excess work to a specialized company or an independent contractor.

47. Safety penalties

PROBLEM: If you are a manufacturer, you are concerned for the safety of your employees and you also want to be sure that you are complying with the numerous and often confusing requirements of The Occupational Safety and Health Act.

DIAGNOSIS: OSHA can indeed seem confusing. Many small businesses are not aware that OSHA provides a free consultation service that can help you assure employee safety and comply with regulations.

PRESCRIPTION: The OSHA consultation begins when the employer requests it and commits to correcting any serious job safety and health hazards that may be identified by the consultant. (If any hazards are discovered by the consultant during this inspection, no citations will be issued and no penalties will be imposed.)

Conducted by state government agencies or universities that employ professional safety and health consultants, the consultation—when conducted at the work site—includes:

- ➲ An opening conference with the employer to explain the ground rules.
- ➲ A walk-through of the workplace to identify specific hazards and to examine aspects of the employer's safety and health program that relate to the scope of the visit.
- ➲ A closing conference.
- ➲ A written report on the consultant's findings and recommendations, sent to the employer.

Besides helping the employer to identify and correct specific hazards, the consultation can provide assistance in developing and implementing effective safety and health programs in the workplace, with emphasis on the prevention of worker injuries and illnesses.

If the employer then corrects all identified hazards and demonstrates that an effective safety and health program is in operation, the company may be exempted from OSHA general schedule enforcement inspections for a period of one year. (This exemption does not apply, however, if there are complaints or if there are accidents to be investigated.)

Consultation Services for the Employer (OSHA publication #3047) contains additional information regarding this free program and a directory of OSHA-funded consultation projects. To obtain a free copy, write to OSHA Office of Information & Consumer Affairs, Room N3637, U.S. Department of Labor, Washington, DC 20210, phone (202) 219-8151.

48. How to disagree with OSHA

PROBLEM: You have just received a citation from OSHA for a safety violation and you do not think it is warranted. How do you fight it?

DIAGNOSIS: Let your objections be heard. If you feel you've received a citation you don't deserve, you are allowed recourse. The key is to document your position accurately and thoroughly.

PRESCRIPTION: Request an informal meeting with OSHA's area director, who has the authority to enter into settlements that revise citations or penalties to avoid prolonged legal disputes. Such a discussion should lead to a resolution.

To learn more about your rights under OSHA, get a free copy of *OSHA Publications and Audiovisual Programs* (OSHA catalog #2019) by sending a self-addressed return envelope to OSHA Publications Office, Room N3101, U.S. Department of Labor, Washington, DC 20210.

49. Managing medically related absences

PROBLEM: An increasing number of government regulations (leaves for childcare, etc.) make it difficult to stabilize the work force, particularly for long-term projects. Such projects often pass through two, three or even four individuals between conception and completion.

DIAGNOSIS: Be prepared for more such government intervention, rather than less, and don't waste time trying to fight it. It's there, and you will be better off learning to live with it.

The best thing you can do is to acquire a thorough understanding of the law and then plan your work and assign your personnel accordingly.

PRESCRIPTION: Under the Family and Medical Leave Act, an employee is entitled to as much as 12 weeks of *unpaid* leave during any 12-month period for any of these reasons:

- The birth of a child.
- Adopting a child.
- Placing a child in foster care.
- A serious health problem.
- Caring for a member of the immediate family (spouse, child or parent) who is suffering from a serious health problem.

Note: The employee must have been employed by this employer for the previous 12-month period and worked at least 1,250 hours during that 12-month period. This act excludes businesses with less than 50 employees within a 75-mile radius.

FMLA also requires that:

- The employer maintain the group health benefits that the employee was receiving at the time such leave began—at the same level and in the same manner as if the employee had continued to work—during the periods of unpaid leave. (The employee may elect to use any accrued *paid* leave—vacation, sick leave, personal leave, etc.—for periods of unpaid FMLA leave.)
- The leave may be taken in blocks of time less than the full 12 weeks on an intermittent or reduced-leave basis. Taking intermittent leave must be approved by the employer, however.
- When the leave is foreseeable, the employee must provide the employer with at least 30 days' notice of the need for the leave.
- In the event the employee claims a serious health condition, the employer may require medical certification of that fact.
- In the event of an employee's serious health condition, the employer may require periodic reports regarding the employee's progress and the employee's intent to return to work during the period of the leave.

- ➲ In certain situations, the employer may require certification that the employee is fit to return to work when the employee does return.

- ➲ When the employee returns from FMLA leave, he or she is entitled to resume the same job. If that job is not available, the employer must place him or her in an equivalent job with equivalent pay, benefits, responsibilities, etc.

- ➲ The employee is not entitled to accrue benefits during the period of unpaid FMLA leave.

50. Successful team building

PROBLEM: You are convinced that teamwork is better than sheer individual effort, particularly when it comes to attacking certain types of business problems, but how do you go about turning a random group of employees into a strong, productive team?

DIAGNOSIS: You should have an outline of what you want the team to accomplish and state those goals outright when you solicit volunteers to serve on the team. Always allow enough flexibility for the team's goals to change because teams tend to take on a life of their own, frequently altering your original vision of their potential.

PRESCRIPTION: Get together with each potential member of the team and find out why he or she has agreed to sign on. Team members' personal agendas tend to affect the outcome of the project.

Try to see that the team includes the proper balance of personalities and that the members have the skills and experience necessary to handle the task(s) you plan to set before them. After the team has been put together:

- ➲ Clearly identify each person's role in the group. This will avoid unnecessary rivalries and prevent time-wasting power plays. It also will ensure that all of the team's major responsibilities will be properly addressed.

- ➲ Give the group a name—an identity. People are more likely to feel that their efforts are important if they belong to a clearly identified, "official" group.

- ➲ Enhance the team's status by publicizing the formation of the group, spelling out the mission of the team and its importance to the company, and reporting regularly on the team's accomplishments.

⊃ Focus on the use of "we" and "our." Such words give everyone the impression that they are a part of the effort and have made a contribution to it.

⊃ The team cannot do its work without adequate information. Provide the team with the background on the project, including why it has become a priority, and see that it has access to whatever other information it needs while it is doing its work.

⊃ Encourage the team to network. Establish how the members will stay in touch and how often. Decide who is authorized to make emergency decisions between meetings.

⊃ Create a relaxed, good-natured atmosphere in which the team can work. Provide refreshments at each meeting and encourage laughter. Have the meetings in a place that is nonthreatening.

⊃ Brainstorm issues in which there are no right or wrong answers and reach decisions by consensus, rather than by vote. Voting is divisive—it makes people take sides.

⊃ Maintain the team philosophy to the end. After the job has been completed, praise the team without singling out individuals. If someone deserves extra praise, take him or her aside for a personal commendation.

51. Basic team requirements

PROBLEM: You have created a number of teams within the company to handle a variety of tasks, but they do not seem to be functioning very effectively. What should you have done differently?

DIAGNOSIS: For optimum effectiveness, teams require five key qualities:

- A sense of mission.
- A need for new challenges.
- An ability to focus on a common goal.
- An awareness of each member's strengths.
- An underlying confidence in each other.

Your role in creating such teams involves:

- Creating favorable performance conditions.
- Building and maintaining the team itself.
- Coaching and helping the team reach its objectives.

PRESCRIPTION: Some of the common mistakes that a leader makes when creating teams and working with the team members include:

- ⮑ Calling the unit a team, but treating the members like individuals.
- ⮑ Failing to set up an enabling structure for the team to work in, such as:
  - Giving the team a well-identified task that will sustain its motivation.
  - Making the team no larger than necessary.
  - Creating a team in which there is a good mix of supplementary and complementary skills and talents.
- ⮑ Not giving the team enough authority to accomplish its task. (Early on, many bosses will give a team too much authority, and later, particularly if the team encounters trouble, they tend to retract the team's authority too quickly.)
- ⮑ Failing to provide a reward incentive for good work.
- ⮑ Failing to provide the team with necessary information.
- ⮑ Failing to train the team properly.
- ⮑ Failing to provide the team with sufficient equipment, space, money and staff to do its work.

Another common fault is to get in the team's way while it is trying to do its work. It is appropriate to intervene at the start of the project (when it is necessary to explain what is expected of the team) and, when necessary, to interrupt the team at some natural break in its work. But don't interrupt the team when it is totally immersed in its work unless there is a crisis to contend with.

52. Avoiding team problems

PROBLEM: Forming teams to tackle various company problems seems simple enough, but the result is often far less than you might expect. Team members bicker. Strong personalities dominate and shy people don't contribute.

DIAGNOSIS: Teams work well in certain situations, in certain companies, for certain individuals—but they're not for everybody.

Before you place too much confidence in the team approach as a means of solving some of your thorniest business problems, you should be aware that this approach often presents some problems of its own.

PRESCRIPTION: Some of the things to watch out for when you consider assigning a problem to a team might include:

⮞ Before a team can be expected to produce satisfactory results, each member of the team should be trained and skilled in the use of:
- Good listening skills.
- Negotiation.
- Leadership.
- Problem-solving.
- Conflict management.
- Group dynamics.
- Self-awareness.
- The value of diversity.
- Risk-taking.
- Customer focus.
- The special talent(s), knowledge or experience that only *he or she* is capable of adding to the team.

⮞ By putting together a team of people from different functions within the company, you immediately make each individual accountable to *two bosses* and make him or her accountable to two potentially opposing sets of goals.

⮞ Even a team needs a leader—ask anybody interested in sports. If there's nobody to set and maintain the direction of the effort, the team is likely to lose its focus and begin wandering aimlessly.

⮞ If you create a team of traditional specialists, you have a *group*, not a *team*. If one of the specialists goes on vacation and nobody can fill in, the team has a basic flaw.

53. Why teams fail

PROBLEM: After creating several teams and watching them approach their work, you've learned that some problems are suited to this approach and some aren't. Some people are suited to working in a team atmosphere and some aren't.

DIAGNOSIS: Teams fail to perform up to expectations for many reasons. Those often cited by people who have been frustrated by the team approach to problem-solving include:

- Decision-making by consensus (the team approach) takes too long.

- Compromise solutions that everyone on the team can accept often produce second-rate answers to the problem.

- Strong individual performers often are not good team members.

- Many people want a "paternalistic" figure who symbolizes wisdom and authority—a strong leader.

- Many team members prefer to work with others who are like themselves and have no appreciation for the value of diversity.

- Stronger, more authoritarian team members tend to take control, and this may stifle the contributions of other members.

PRESCRIPTION: The trick to creating a successful team is to recognize when the circumstances are right for using the team approach and when they are not. For example, teams often function poorly when deadlines are short or lots of evidence is missing. Be sure to: 1) carefully select team members whose skills and experiences are complementary; 2) train team members thoroughly before beginning; and 3) monitor the team's progress regularly.

- Don't expect quick decisions and be sure to allow adequate time for the team to function.

- Don't assign tasks to a team which can be performed better by an individual.

54. When performance is below par

PROBLEM: One of your employees is performing poorly, and you can't quite put your finger on the reason for it.

DIAGNOSIS: Rather than concentrate on the employee's poor performance, it's often better to try to uncover the underlying reason for the poor performance. Poor performance may be caused by a flagging interest in the job or assignment, or it may be caused by some personal situation not involved with work.

PRESCRIPTION: To trace the *reason* for an employee's poor performance, try to answer these questions:

➲ Exactly what is the nature of the problem?

➲ Does the employee have basic self-management skills:
  • Organizing.
  • Prioritizing.
  • Meeting deadlines.
  If not, formal training courses can teach those skills.

➲ Does the employee have the technical skills to do the job? If not, teach him or her the skills and assign a mentor to review work and provide ongoing coaching.

➲ Does the employee have the ability to learn the work? If not, transfer him or her to some other job or consider termination.

➲ Does the employee possess the interpersonal skills necessary to establish and maintain effective work relationships? If not, train or coach him or her in those skills. If neither works, consider termination.

➲ Does the employee have the necessary tools to do the work? If not, provide them or work around them.

➲ Does the employee have a positive incentive for doing the work correctly and on schedule? If not, build them into your system. At the very least remove the *dis*incentives and make sure the employee understands how his or her work contributes to the overall goals of the company.

Here are some other steps to take to help the employee get back on track.

➲ Talk to the employee and compare his recent performance with your concept of *superior* performance.

➲ If the employee doesn't seem to catch on or seems indifferent, he or she may be beyond hope.

➲ If the employee's response involves blame or denial, you have gained his or her attention and you can continue to provide feedback that will encourage better performance.

➲ If the employee's response seems thoughtful and receptive, you probably can work toward improving his or her performance.

➲ Don't expect the matter to change after a single interview. Set a reasonable time limit in your mind on when you expect to see some improvement in the employee's behavior and on when you expect to see him or her achieve a complete turnaround. If those deadlines come and go without change, more drastic action may be needed.

55. Correcting behavioral problems

PROBLEM: An employee is disrupting your operation with bad behavior. In addition to setting a poor example, this employee is demoralizing many of the other workers.

DIAGNOSIS: What exactly is the nature of the employee's bad behavior? Is it serious or merely annoying? If it's merely irritating, caution the employee that the behavior is inappropriate, that he or she should make changes immediately and that you will take disciplinary measures otherwise.

PRESCRIPTION: Ask yourself these questions:

- ➲ If there are rules about such conduct, is the employee aware of them? If there are no rules, establish some— including a set of consequences for those who disobey them. If there are rules, but the employee is not aware of them, see that he or she learns of them.
- ➲ Is the employee's behavior critical to the organization or to the safety and well-being of other employees? If so, stop the offensive behavior at once, then decide upon the disciplinary action to be taken.
- ➲ Does the employee's behavior undermine your authority or the basic supervisor/subordinate relationship? If so, you should consider terminating the offender.
- ➲ Is the behavior deliberate? If so, take action that is strong enough to deter others from imitating it.

Maintain a written record of offenses, conversations with the offender, threatened disciplinary action and action taken in response to the poor behavior. Appropriate disciplinary action, other than termination, might include:

- Having a reprimand documented on the employee's job-performance records.
- Moving the employee to a lesser position.
- Suspension without pay.

56. Addressing discrimination

PROBLEM: You have discovered that some of your employees do not seem to be accepting new employees—especially those who are female, Black or Hispanic.

DIAGNOSIS: It is hard to believe that such conditions still exist in modern business. Unfortunately, they do, and they can lead to serious business and legal difficulties if they are allowed to continue.

PRESCRIPTION: After you have determined precisely what conditions exist, be sure all of your employees are familiar with the company's policy regarding discrimination.

Sometimes, it is beneficial to arrange for positive experiences between people of diverse cultures, enabling each to learn more about, and hence better understand, the background of the other. Such events can include company-sponsored cookouts, musical interludes, movies, lectures and other activities of a multicultural nature.

In specific cases, be sure the employee is not being rejected because of behavior that is irritating to the others, rather than because of prejudices related to race, sex or nationality. Encourage all employees to work harmoniously.

- ⮑ Be sure to follow up promptly on any reports of bias.

- ⮑ Get all of the facts before you reach any conclusions or take any corrective action. Talk to the individual who has made an allegation of bias, get the names of the individuals accused and of any witnesses. Interview each of them.

- ⮑ If you believe the accused is innocent, talk to the person who made the accusation and explain why you feel he or she may have misunderstood the situation. Advise him or her of his right to file a complaint, if he or she chooses to do so.

- ⮑ If you believe the accusation to be true, take corrective action, even if it means terminating the offender.

57. Dealing with sexual harassment

PROBLEM: Sexual harassment has become the buzzword in many companies today. Many employers are biting their nails for fear that some employee, somewhere, is intimidating someone in an inappropriate manner, without their knowledge. The first news they receive may be a court summons.

DIAGNOSIS: Your concern is well-founded. Under the Civil Rights Act of 1991, a company with fewer than 100 workers can be required to pay up to $50,000 in damages as a result of a sexual harassment case.

The Equal Employment Opportunity Commission (EEOC) says: "Unwelcome sexual advances, requests for sexual favors, and other verbal or physical conduct of a sexual nature constitute sexual harassment when: 1) submission to such conduct is made either explicitly or implicitly a term or condition of an individual's employment; 2) submission to or rejection of such conduct by an individual is used as the basis for employment decisions affecting such individual; or 3) such conduct has the purpose or effect of unreasonably interfering with an individual's work performance or creating an intimidating, hostile, or offensive working environment."

"Creating a hostile environment" involves a worker who acts in a way that is offensive or intimidating to another—and your company can be held liable for that if you know about the conduct and do nothing to stop it.

Your company also can be held liable if one of your workers harasses another by exacting sexual favors in exchange for employment or advancement (*quid pro quo* harassment).

Getting employees to understand that they can report harassment without fear of reprisals is difficult.

PRESCRIPTION: You can discourage sexual harassment in your company in a variety of ways:

➲ Adopt a sexual harassment policy, promising that grievances will be quickly and thoroughly investigated.

➲ Spell out the disciplinary measures that will be taken against anyone who harasses another employee. Also spell out what action will be taken against those who bring false charges of sexual harassment.

➲ Create a "neutral" and nonthreatening body to which employees will feel safe bringing their complaints.

➲ Investigate charges promptly.

➲ Take all complaints seriously.

➲ Take appropriate action, being sure that you never allow a complaining party to feel that he/she has been treated in an offhanded manner.

Call for the EEOC's free *Sexual Harassment Package*, which contains a fact sheet, the EEOC's sexual harassment guidelines for employers and the guidelines for determining what constitutes sexual harassment.

58. Communication between the sexes

PROBLEM: Many of the men in your company are petrified over the fear that they will say or do something that could be construed as harassment. Your female employees may feel intimidated by the "locker-room humor" that often pervades the workplace. Sexual jokes or comments may cause discomfort, even if no harassment is intended.

DIAGNOSIS: No question, this is a thorny problem, and one without any simple, one-size-fits-all solution.

As more women join the employment ranks—and more women become bosses—both men and women are learning that there are different communication styles between the sexes.

PRESCRIPTION: This is no one-way street. Women as well as men must adjust the way in which they think, speak and act in various situations.

Men need to:

- Think about women as business beings, rather than sexual beings.
- Recognize that a woman is as unique in her gender group as a man is in his.
- Communicate with women individually, rather than as members of a stereotypical group.
- Realize that the impact of a communication may be bad, even if the intent was good.
- Eliminate sexual humor and use general humor, including self-put-down humor.
- Learn to say or do *nothing* if the meaning is in doubt.

Women need to:

- Remain objective when trying to express their feelings, rather than be branded as overemotional.
- Express their feelings verbally, rather than nonverbally, because men often have difficulty with reading behavior.
- Forego "male-bashing" as unproductive.
- Use more humor, but not self-effacing humor.
- Say what needs to be said concisely, avoiding excessive apologies and disclaimers.
- Recognize that men often do not understand the impact of their sexually related comments. If such a comment offends you, say something at the time it occurs, and then forget it.

59. Personality clashes

PROBLEM: A couple of your employees have started bickering between themselves, causing other employees to take sides in the debate. The entire affair has become quite disruptive to productivity and is affecting employee morale.

DIAGNOSIS: A harmonious working environment is every employer's goal—and one that is too often elusive. Even so, there are various levels of discord, and in some situations, a little well-intended competitiveness among the employees can even be beneficial.

PRESCRIPTION: Determine the exact nature of the problem. If it isn't important to the effectiveness of the operation, try to live with it.

- ➲ If the situation worsens or is critical to your business, talk to the offender(s).
- ➲ If it is important for you to maintain good relations with that individual, try not to be confrontational or force him or her to change. Try to work out some resolution.
- ➲ If continuing relations with the individual are not particularly important, see if you can't offer some incentive that might encourage a change of behavior.
- ➲ Try to avoid disciplinary action if at all possible—*unless* the offensive behavior is (or becomes) a genuine threat to your business.

60. Getting rid of your mistakes

PROBLEM: You have a real troublemaker in your organization, but you are afraid to resort to termination for fear the employee may take you to court for wrongful dismissal.

DIAGNOSIS: These days, many employers are concerned about the cost and the legal problems that may be associated with dismissing an employee—and for good reason.

To legally establish "just cause" for termination, an employer must prove serious misconduct or incompetence and show that the employee was given sufficient opportunity to correct his or her problems.

PRESCRIPTION: The best way to avoid the costs and legal difficulties that can be involved in a wrongful dismissal suit is to base your company policies on the current legal trends within your jurisdiction. Consult a legal expert when you develop these policies.

Most jurisdictions have some sort of legislation that spells out the minimum periods of notice that an employer must extend to an employee before dismissal.

If "just cause" has been established, the employer does not have to give the employee any notice.

What constitutes just cause?

- ➲ Refusal to carry out lawful and reasonable orders.
- ➲ Dishonesty, especially when the individual has been caught in the act.
- ➲ Insolence—but only if it can be proven that the employee's conduct was of such an insulting and insubordinate nature as to make continued employment impossible.
- ➲ Conflict with the employer's interest if it can be shown that such conduct carries with it an air of deceit and a lack of fidelity.
- ➲ Conduct outside of normal working hours if actual or potential detriment to the employer can be shown.
- ➲ Incompetence—if you can document it and show that the employee has been notified of the problem and warned that dismissal will result if he or she does not meet the expected level of performance.

What does not constitute just cause?

- ➲ Intoxication or habitual drunkenness is not grounds for immediate dismissal because the courts usually rule that the employee should first be warned that dismissal can occur if the drinking problem continues.
- ➲ Illness is not just cause unless it can be proven that the illness is permanent and the employee will not be able to return to work.

61. When you need to cut back production

PROBLEM: One of your production units has become obsolete and it is not worth updating to current standards. Unfortunately, to close it will require dislocating a number of employees.

DIAGNOSIS: Once again, there are government regulations that require you to take specific steps in any situation involving the closing of a facility and the dislocation of some employees. These regulations are outlined in the Worker Adjustment and Retraining Act (WARA).

PRESCRIPTION: This federal regulation does not apply to the closing of temporary facilities or when the layoffs of personnel are caused by the closing of a faltering company, unforeseeable business circumstances or a natural disaster. But it does apply when the facility is shut down for more than six months and when 50 or more workers lose their jobs as a result during a 30-day period. The act also covers mass layoffs in which: 1) 500 or more workers; or 2) 33 percent or more of the employer's work force are laid off for a period of six months or longer.

Under WARA, the employer must provide the workers with notice 60 days in advance of the closing and the attendant layoffs. The notice must be provided to affected workers *or their representatives (union)*, to the state dislocated worker unit, and the appropriate local government.

Write to the U.S. Department of Labor, Employment and Training Administration, Office of Work-Based Learning, Room N-4469, 200 Constitution Ave. NW, Washington, DC 20210, for a pamphlet entitled *A Guide to Advance Notice of Closings and Layoffs*.

62. How to sell an unpopular idea

PROBLEM: Eventually, it becomes necessary to make some major changes in your company and your employees don't seem to like them. What can you do?

DIAGNOSIS: In my book *Rate Yourself As a Manager* (Prentice-Hall, Inc.), I list some ways in which you can help to reduce your employees' resistance to change and sell a new plan, no matter how unpopular it may seem at first.

PRESCRIPTION: To help you implement change, realize that others may not share your beliefs or approve of your attitudes. Also realize that many of their beliefs and attitudes are the result of past habits and patterns. With that in mind, here are a few things you can try:

- Visualize the change from the standpoint of those who will have to use or adapt to it.
- Anticipate the difficulties that may arise in gaining acceptance for your program and devise ways to make the transition more acceptable.
- Carefully consider all of the consequences of the proposed change. Tell your employees what will be different and explain why.
- Provide as much forewarning as possible.

➲ Make the change(s) gradually, one step at a time. Avoid surprises. Abrupt, sweeping changes can be disruptive—even dangerous.

➲ Be willing to bend and modify your plan where small points are involved.

➲ Find out what others want and then see if you can modify the plan to satisfy those needs without sacrificing any of the main points in your program.

➲ See if you can offer your employees some incentive to change.

➲ If you must reduce an employee's responsibilities or function, use something physical, such as a desk, telephone or the like, to raise their status.

➲ Talk with key people and enlist their support for the change.

➲ Find out who is most likely to be rebellious, and put these individuals in charge of implementing the change.

➲ As the change is being made, stay in communication with the employees.

63. Stopping the rumor mill

PROBLEM: Rumors have been circulating wildly throughout your company. Some have the firm being sold, some have it going broke and others have it being absorbed by your biggest competitor. None of these rumors are true, but how do you stop the rumor mill?

DIAGNOSIS: Realize that people are going to think and talk about things that affect them and their jobs. Some executives actually encourage the rumor mill by adopting a secretive attitude, giving rise to speculation.

PRESCRIPTION: Decide if it's really *important* to keep the topic under speculation a secret, or if it's even *possible* to keep it a secret. Never try to keep something hidden unless you have a good, valid reason to do so.

➲ If secrecy is vital, try giving your employees some legitimate work-related news to talk about as a means of diverting their attention from your secret.

➲ If it's not, put the facts on the table promptly and make them available to everybody.

64. When employees strike

PROBLEM: Your employees are on strike, your inventories have been exhausted and your customers are being wooed by the competition.

DIAGNOSIS: Begin by getting a clear picture of the situation. Gather the facts and attempt to develop an understanding of the emotional state of your striking employees. Only after that will you be in a position to initiate an effective counterattack.

PRESCRIPTION: Assemble the pertinent facts: the current wage and benefit levels, the history of past negotiations and what the company's last offer was. Get the same background on the non-economic portions of the contract, such as work rules, grievances, representation, overtime, etc.

Learn about the political forces at work in the union and the power structure behind the strike. If there is any rancor between the bargaining teams, do whatever is necessary to reduce the tension.

Begin the dialogue

- Hold a meeting with the bargaining agents, avoiding publicity.
- Demonstrate your willingness to bargain.
- Assess their attitudes and positions firsthand.
- Determine what pressures they are under.
- Try to establish how strong their resolve is and how deep their hostility runs.
- Explain the company's objectives.
- Say that you want to reopen negotiations and keep the lines of communications open while both sides try to reach a settlement.
- Make it very clear that you are their last hope for an early settlement.
- Be sure to underscore the necessity to keep the company competitive—*or there will be no jobs in the future*.
- Be respectful of their needs and their bargaining posture.
- Make no concessions, but look for common ground.
- Prepare the union leaders for another visit.

Assess your position

➲ Isolate the issues that divide the two sides and identify the ones that are essential to reaching an agreement.

➲ Assign dollar amounts to the offers that may resolve the key issues.

➲ Identify any areas in which rejecting your offer would give a strong advantage to your competitors.

➲ Noneconomic issues are more difficult to negotiate than economic ones, so concentrate on the few that are vital to you and forget about the others temporarily.

➲ Study your negotiating team. If there is any bad chemistry there, change some assignments to eliminate it. Increase the roles of those who seem most likely to get results.

Develop an offer

➲ Package the economic offers that you can tolerate with any noneconomic gains that you can realistically hope to achieve.

➲ If the cost is going to be high and an economic recession is at hand, seek a short-term agreement. Perhaps you will be able to negotiate more favorably next year.

➲ Focus on the numbers that you need to settle upon and the amount of negotiating room that is available.

➲ Keep the number of "deal-breaker" items to a minimum. Be sure the union knows what yours are, and be sure that you know theirs.

Resume negotiations

➲ Test your offer quietly and in general terms with the union before scheduling a formal meeting. Get a sense of how it will be received in advance. If it appears that the offer will be rejected immediately, hold off on scheduling a formal meeting.

➲ Don't expect any commitments at the premeeting session, just an idea of their attitude and receptivity.

➲ If their response seems favorable, schedule a meeting and put your offer on the table.

➲ Emphasize how serious the situation is and how favorably the new offer compares with contracts at competing firms.

- ➲ Stress that yours is an offer born from crisis, not one that necessarily is best for everyone in the long term.
- ➲ Sell your proposal, be flexible but determined, and be alert to the bargaining committee's response.
- ➲ End the stalemate, resume negotiations and try to find a mutually acceptable answer.

Reach an agreement

- ➲ Be sure the union leadership will recommend ratification of the agreement and work for its approval. Although it is the union's job to sell the contract, you can help by permitting balloting on company premises, allowing workers to return to work before formal ratification and avoiding mention of any disciplinary measures.
- ➲ Do not gloat over any concessions you have won and ignore any signs of union glee over the concessions you have made.
- ➲ Do not comment publicly about any part of the agreement until it has been officially approved.

Get ready for the next round

- ➲ This is the time to be thinking about the position you want to be in when the next round of negotiations rolls around. Put together a plan for getting there.

65. The end of the line

PROBLEM: No matter how hard you have tried to work things out with an employee, irreconcilable differences make it absolutely necessary for you to resort to termination.

DIAGNOSIS: A company that hires the right people and manages them properly does little firing, but releasing your mistakes is inevitable. No one benefits by continuing a mismatch.

PRESCRIPTION: Never take a dismissal lightly. Remember that the individual you let go probably has friends among the other employees, among your suppliers, among your customers and even among your competitors. Do not handle the termination in such a way as to damage your image or reputation with the bystanders.

➲ Preventive medicine may help you to avoid subsequent dismissals. Let your employees know what you expect of them *before* a misunderstanding occurs.

➲ Create an early-warning system, such as an annual performance appraisal, to alert you when things are not going smoothly.

➲ If you uncover something wrong and find a way to fix it, you may possibly eliminate the need to terminate an employee.

➲ Include the employee when analyzing the problem. Let him or her evaluate himself. If your employee acknow- ledges the problem, you are one step closer to resolving it. If he or she denies it, you have additional ammunition if it becomes necessary to terminate, and support for your action if he or she should decide to sue for unjust or discriminatory treatment.

➲ If a termination is unavoidable, document every action carefully. Be very specific, both in your conversations and in your memos. Describe specific instances that have led up to the dismissal; don't generalize. See that the employee receives a copy of every memo that goes into his or her personnel file.

➲ Act quickly. Once a decision to terminate has been reached, don't procrastinate. Be sure to follow all of the company policies to preclude legal action.

➲ Make a checklist of points to discuss with the employee during an exit interview. Be candid about the reason for the termination, and have someone else present to witness what was said and the employee's reaction to it.

➲ Major topics to discuss during the exit interview should include:

  • Will the employee receive severance pay? Assistance in hunting a job? Good references?

  • How long will his or her company health insurance bene- fits last? What will they cost? Are they convertible?

  • Will the employee be eligible for unemployment benefits?

➲ During the exit interview, collect any company property that the employee may have, such as keys to the office.

➲ If the termination is relatively amicable, you might consider helping the employee find another job. This needn't entail hiring an expensive placement firm; you could simply inform vendors, customers or others in the industry that the employee is available. In some cases, you might furnish the employee with a formal introduction to potential employers. For a time, you might consider letting him or her use the resources of the office (desk, telephone, etc.) during the job-hunt.

➲ Immediately begin the search for someone to replace the employee.

➲ Think about the concerns of the other employees. The way in which you handle this individual will be seen as a reflection of the way in which you might one day handle them.

➲ Do a postmortem. See if something could have been done to preclude terminating the employee. If so, try not to make the same mistake again.

Chapter 7

Motivating employees

66. When motivation is missing

PROBLEM: Your employees seem to be lacking in motivation.

DIAGNOSIS: Perhaps you have not been responding to the things that tend to produce a lack of motivation.

PRESCRIPTION: By understanding what it is that causes people to *lose* their motivation, you may be in a better position to prevent such things from occurring.
People tend to lose their motivation when:

- ➲ You fail to give them your full attention.
- ➲ You fail to acknowledge their personal preferences.
- ➲ You belittle their accomplishments.
- ➲ You criticize them in front of others.
- ➲ You are insensitive to time schedules.
- ➲ You do not complete your share of the work.
- ➲ You are preoccupied with your own projects.
- ➲ You are prone to showing favoritism.

Avoid these counterproductive habits and you may find that your employees show a marked increase in motivation.

67. Tapping into attitudes

PROBLEM: The same old complaints and morale problems keep surfacing week after week.

DIAGNOSIS: The most knowledgeable people about working conditions are currently on your payroll: the employees. Why not give them the opportunity to provide input on ways to improve the operation of your company?

PRESCRIPTION: Consider a survey of all employees every six months. It should be designed to develop information on at least four key topics:

- ⮑ Morale.
- ⮑ The company's upper management:
  - Employee support.
  - Ability to articulate its goals.
  - Attentiveness to employees' ideas.
  - Fairness.
- ⮑ The employee's immediate supervisor:
  - Coaching.
  - Listening.
  - Praising.
  - Responsiveness.
- ⮑ Core values.

The company guarantees each employee's confidentiality in order to garner honest and objective answers to its questions.

After the survey has been taken, the company:

- ⮑ Gives each manager a summary of the company-wide responses plus a summary of the responses given by his or her own subordinates.
- ⮑ Encourages managers to use the material as a means of correcting their own shortcomings.
- ⮑ Makes sure that any thorny problems don't get buried and forgotten.

Within a month, traditional top-down appraisals are conducted between the managers and their subordinates. In this way, the company underscores its belief that everyone can improve his or her performance and everyone should have an opportunity to show how that will happen.

68. Providing opportunity to perform

PROBLEM: It often seems like your employees lack enthusiasm for their work, don't try to do things better and need to be told what to do and how to do it every time a situation arises.

DIAGNOSIS: Your employees may be afraid of the consequences of doing something wrong. They need to be given more freedom, more praise and less criticism.

PRESCRIPTION: There are several things that you can do to stimulate greater involvement by your employees:

- ⮆ Reward communication and cooperation between the employees.
- ⮆ Set a good example by seeing that your employees get all of the information they need—and soon enough to enable them to make intelligent decisions regarding their work.
- ⮆ Make sure the employees clearly understand your plans and goals.
- ⮆ Encourage employees to use those plans and goals as the basis for doing their daily work.
- ⮆ Be sure your employees feel free to ask questions or express their opinions without fear of a put-down or a reprisal.
- ⮆ Never punish individual initiative that yields improvement.

69. Getting better ideas from employees

PROBLEM: You have learned over the years that your employees have a lot of good ideas for ways in which to improve the business and make it more productive and/or more profitable. Lately, however, the number of incoming employee suggestions has fallen away to a trickle.

Is there a way to revitalize the employee suggestion program?

DIAGNOSIS: Often, a good program will grow stale, not because it's no longer worthwhile, but because people have grown too accustomed to it. It has become old hat.

Try to give your program a new look and see if the response doesn't improve.

PRESCRIPTION: Florida Power & Light Co. put new life into its employee suggestion program by attaching a form to the back of each work order. Whenever a crew completes the paperwork for a job, it comes across this question: "Do you have any suggestion for how this job might have been done better?"

Every suggestion is acknowledged by a supervisor within 24 hours, and a decision regarding its disposition is given to the employee within 72 hours.

Employees receive points for any suggestion that is implemented, and the points can be redeemed for prizes from a catalog containing a variety of items. The employee's name and suggestion are then displayed prominently in areas where other employees can see them.

70. What the best need most

PROBLEM: Lately, some of your best people have left the company and taken jobs elsewhere.

DIAGNOSIS: Too often, people tend to think that this occurs because the departing employee has gotten more money or will have a more prominent position elsewhere—but money and titles aren't the whole story.

PRESCRIPTION: Look for the "hidden causes" of employee discontent. Here are a few things to watch:

- ➲ Work rules are too rigid.
- ➲ Expectation is not clear.
- ➲ Jobs are dead ended.
- ➲ Seniority prevails over performance.
- ➲ People are not adequately trained.

71. How to handle an overachiever

PROBLEM: On your staff are a couple of individuals who, because they are ambitious, because they are nonconformists and because they are not afraid to speak their minds on important issues, are considered by others within the company to be irritating and presumptuous.

DIAGNOSIS: Indeed, overachievers can appear to be brash and, to certain people, even threatening. Nonetheless, handled properly, they can be some of your most effective workers.

PRESCRIPTION: There are some very effective ways to deal with overachievers, including:

➲ Delegate some of your more challenging and pressure-laden tasks to them (under careful supervision). That will enable them to perform a valuable service and acquire some new skills at the same time.

➲ Provide them with assignments that challenge their capabilities and provide a release for their energies, at the same time allowing them to exercise skills that will be essential for future promotions.

➲ Give them temporary assignments to test their abilities and to see how well they will respond under pressure.

➲ Test their flexibility to see how quickly and effectively they can adjust when solving a problem or faced with an opportunity.

➲ Praise (and reward) them publicly to ensure their continuing loyalty. Such individuals often are more driven by the need for ego gratification than by a desire for titles or bonuses.

72. What keeps morale up?

PROBLEM: You often get the feeling that your employees go through their workdays like robots—unfeeling, unseeing, unmotivated and unproductive.

DIAGNOSIS: Somehow, the pizzazz has gone out of their work. This frequently happens, especially when the work is dull and repetitive.

PRESCRIPTION: There are some things that an employer can do to pep up the personnel. Among them:

➲ Allow employees to work flexible hours (obviously not an option for certain workers).

➲ Encourage employees to continue their education by establishing a tuition reimbursement program when: 1) classes are completed; and 2) a passing grade is received.

➲ Discourage absenteeism by paying employees for any unused sick days.

- ⮑ Set departmental goals that can serve as a challenge to the employees and an incentive for them to be more productive, especially if exceeding those goals has been linked to an incentive program.

- ⮑ Publicly praise workers who do well.

- ⮑ Create in-house training programs that will enable employees to gain the skills necessary to earn more money and/or promotions.

- ⮑ Devise games that involve friendly competition in areas needing improvement.

73. How *not* to lose your best people

PROBLEM: You have attempted to hire and train the best people available but, recognizing this, your competitors have been systematically trying to lure some of your employees away.

DIAGNOSIS: Good people are the backbone of your organization and they represent a sizable investment in training and development. In my book *Rate Your Executive Potential* (John Wiley & Sons, Inc., 1988), I list six ways in which a company can protect itself from the ravages of raiders.

PRESCRIPTION: Good employees will be hesitant to leave your company if you:

- ⮑ Focus on their performance and not on their seniority.

- ⮑ Don't make your work rules too rigid.

- ⮑ Avoid arbitrary cutbacks.

- ⮑ Provide opportunity for personal growth and avoid creating dead-ended jobs.

- ⮑ Provide targeted, specific goals.

- ⮑ Reward real accomplishment and not mediocrity.

Chapter 8

Paying for performance

74. How to link pay to performance

PROBLEM: Every time the company passes out a raise, you hear a chorus of moaning and groaning. One person got too much, another got too little, the "most deserving" got none at all.

DIAGNOSIS: It's never easy to decide how much of a raise to give to whom and on what basis. And if you do so without a specific rationale in mind, you'll not only hear a lot of complaints, but you'll probably find that you've wasted a lot of money as well.

PRESCRIPTION: The most satisfactory programs usually are those that tie an employee's raise to performance on the job during the period under review. That is the surest way to see that top performers are recognized, and those who are simply going through the motions are given an incentive to work harder.

Some tips about awarding raises:

- ➲ Put the amount in perspective. If it is lower than usual, explain why.
- ➲ Don't be defensive. Never apologize for giving someone a raise.
- ➲ Combine raises with feedback. While you are distributing the raises, tell the employees what you are doing and why. Top performers will appreciate the recognition; under-achievers need to know why they are receiving a smaller raise.
- ➲ Set clear objectives for the year ahead so that employees will know precisely what they have to do to earn a raise during the coming year.

⊃ Review an individual's performance broadly. Always tie the raise to overall performance, not to some isolated success. Use bonuses to reward one-time achievements.

⊃ Do not tie strings to the raise. A raise provides positive reinforcement to those who have done good work. To suggest that it carries with it an obligation to work extra hours or carry a heavier workload defeats the purpose.

75. The unconventional approach

PROBLEM: You're looking for an equitable way to compensate your employees, but you don't know of a fair way to determine who is performing a more valuable service to the company—the man who operates a drill press or the woman who keeps your books.

DIAGNOSIS: Many pay systems actually hinder the recognition of exceptional performance because they are based on:

• How long the employee has been with the company.
• How much the cost of living has increased during the past year.
• How many people a person supervises.
• What other people in the organization are being paid.
• What other companies are paying for comparable work.
• How "clean" (or "dirty") the job is.

PRESCRIPTION: Instead of focusing on individual compensation, which often has the effect of pitting one employee against another, find ways to reward teamwork and collaboration.

Reconsider merit raises that merely increase your costs without compensating you with better performance or the acquisition of any new skills. Instead, put more dollars into programs that offer variable pay. Some possibilities to consider:

⊃ Business plan gain-sharing. This approach typically focuses on productivity and quality. An example is a company that allows its employees to share half of the cost savings if the company can beat its budgeted cost-per-pound of product during a specified performance period.

⊃ Win-sharing. This technique is based on measuring performance against profit, quality, customer value and productivity. The reward, which is shared equally by all members of the team, is based on a predetermined goal established for the current fiscal year.

Some companies will deduct funds from the win-sharing pot if warranty claims exceed the planned level, which helps to establish the point that quality is a major concern in the company.

➲ Group variable pay. One company uses this approach, which is funded by financial and qualitative results, for managers. To earn an award, the entire organization must work together to cut costs, boost productivity and improve customer satisfaction.

76. Rewarding lower-paid employees

PROBLEM: The company does not want to neglect the front line people. What's the best approach?

DIAGNOSIS: Lower-income workers are inclined to the philosophy that "a bird in the hand is worth two in the bush." Their needs tend to be short-range, and they usually prefer immediate rewards to long-term promises.

PRESCRIPTION: Generally speaking, the low-income employee will prefer a cash bonus to a stock option. Stock ownership does not offer an immediate reward for doing good work.

➲ Other incentives favored by low-wage employees are paid vacations, days off, discounts on merchandise, gifts of merchandise and things of that nature.

➲ Some companies award points to employees who do outstanding work. The points can then be exchanged for various items of merchandise, selected from a catalog.

77. Bonuses: blessing or curse?

PROBLEM: The company can't afford to give a raise to every employee, so you have decided to award bonuses to selected employees as an alternative.

DIAGNOSIS: A bonus will achieve the same purpose as a raise, especially during an economic downturn, and that is to encourage exceptional performance.

Employees should never be made to feel that they deserve a raise or a bonus simply because a given timespan has elapsed. They should be made to feel that such rewards are earned through consistent, determined, purposeful work.

PRESCRIPTION: Bonuses serve their purpose best when they are awarded throughout the year, and they are most effective when they are given out as soon as possible after the event for which they are being awarded.

➲ Never make bonuses an automatic occurrence.

➲ A bonus can be a real stimulant to overworked employees who are working on a horrendous project, who have been working under particularly difficult conditions or who have been laboring against an extremely difficult deadline.

78. Stock options offer strong incentives

PROBLEM: The company is on the verge of great growth. To retain—and reward—your key people, you would like to establish a stock option program.

DIAGNOSIS: Few things offer as much incentive as a well-conceived and well-executed stock option plan for employees. It shows them that you appreciate their contributions and that you recognize them as important members of your team. At the same time, such plans tend to discourage key employees from capitalizing on their success in your company by going someplace else.

Stock option plans that tie stock to performance and spread the wealth as widely as possible are particularly well-suited to knowledge-driven companies that are looking for a new way to motivate the staff.

PRESCRIPTION: A stock option gives you the right to purchase a specific *number of shares* of the company's stock at a specific *price* within a specific *period of time*. You do not *have* to buy the shares, but you *may* buy the shares—as you choose.

There are a number of ways to go about creating a stock option plan. Some plans offer options only to top executives, while others offer options to everyone in the firm. Options generally are—or eventually become—a negotiable part of an employee's total compensation package.

Stock appreciation rights

Under this option, the employee does not actually buy the shares of company stock, but he benefits from any appreciation in the stock's value.

With this type of program, the employee does not have to put up any cash of his own in order to exercise his option.

Restricted stock

Under the terms of some stock option programs, the employer gives or sells stock to the employee *on the condition that the employee will work for the employer for a specified period of time.* The transaction is not considered "compensation" until the stock has been vested, at which time the employee must declare the value of the stock as ordinary income.

Section 83(b) of the Internal Revenue Service code allows you to include in income the *difference* between the fair market value of the stock *on the date the stock is purchased* and the cost of the stock *at the time the restricted stock is actually issued.* This amount is then taxed *as ordinary income* in the year in which the stock is issued.

In order to be eligible for the IRS election, the stock must be received by the employee in connection with "performing a service" (that is, doing his or her job), and he or she must exercise the election within 30 days of receiving the restricted stock.

Example: You agree to sell an employee 1,000 shares of stock (currently valued at $25 per share) for just $10 a share on the condition that he or she must work for the company for a period of five years.

If the employee's employment is terminated for any reason during that five-year period, the employee must sell the shares back to the company for $10 per share.

If the employee continues to work for the company for the required five-year period, however, the stock becomes his or hers, and the employee then must report the sum of $15,000 ($15 appreciation in value x 1,000 shares) as ordinary income that year on his income tax.

Incentive Stock Options (ISO)

In another type of program, the Incentive Stock Option, the employee is not required to pay tax on the stock until he or she eventually *sells* or *exchanges it for more than he or she paid for it.* If the shares are held for a specified period of time, the profits can be taxed as a "capital gain."

One advantage to this type of program is that the employee does not have to pay any tax on the shares until he or she *actually realizes a gain on them,* and the profit can often be treated as a capital gain, which is taxed more favorably than ordinary income.

ISOs offer some other advantages as well, but there also are some restrictions:

➲ Employee status: From the day the employee receives the ISO until three months before he or she exercises it, he or she must be employed by the company granting it or a related company. This means that, if the employee so chooses, he or she can exercise the option up to three months *after leaving the company*. If the employee leaves the company because of permanent and total disability, however—and the employer's plan allows it—he or she can have *up to one year* to exercise the ISO.

    If the employee should die, ISOs pass on to his or her beneficiaries and they may exercise them.

➲ Option period: Unless the employee owns more than 10 percent of the company's stock, he or she must exercise an ISO within 10 years of the date it is granted. If the employee owns more than 10 percent of the stock, the deadline may not exceed five years.

    The company must grant ISOs within 10 years of the date the shareholders formally approve the stock option plan or the plan is adopted, whichever occurs soonest.

➲ Fair market price: The option price cannot be less than the fair market price of the stock on the date the option is granted. If an employee owns more than 10 percent of the company stock, however, a special rule applies, setting the fair market value at *least 110 percent of the fair market value* on the date the ISO is granted.

➲ $100,000 ceiling: Since 1986, no more than $100,000 worth of stock (valued at the time the ISO was granted) can be exercised for the first time in any one year. This does not limit the amount of stock the employer can grant an employee; rather, it limits the amount of stock that the employee can exercise in any one year.

➲ Order of exercise: Employees must exercise any ISOs granted to them prior to 1987 in the order in which they were granted. Any ISOs granted *after* 1986 may be exercised in any order employees wish.

➲ Capital gains: An employee can claim long-term capital gains on the sale of stock bought through ISOs only if he or she holds the shares for two years from the date the option was granted *or* more than one year from the date the shares actually were transferred to the employee, whichever is later. Otherwise, the gain will be taxed as ordinary income.

◗ Transfers: Only the employee and his or her heirs can exercise these ISOs, and the employee cannot contribute his or her options to an IRA or other type of retirement plan.

Only the employee can exercise his options during his lifetime, and options cannot be assigned in a divorce settlement. The employee cannot sell the right to exercise an option or use that right as collateral for a loan.

Nonqualified Stock Options (NQO)

When an employee exercises this type of option, there is generally an immediate tax bite, plus another bite when he or she later sells the stock at a profit.

Example: Assume you grant your employee an NQO to buy 1,000 shares of stock (currently valued at $25 per share) for just $10 a share. At the time the employee exercises this option, the IRS will tax him or her on the difference between the option price ($10) and the market price ($25). In other words, the employee will be taxed on $15,000 (1,000 shares x $15 per share), which will be treated as ordinary income. If the stock goes up to $40 per share over the next two years and the employee decides to sell the shares, he or she will be taxed again—this time, on the $15,000 profit ($40 sale price - $25 purchase price x 1,000 shares). For tax purposes, the profit will be treated as a capital gain.

The Securities and Exchange Commission imposes certain special rules on corporate "insiders" (officers, directors and those who own more than 10 percent of the company stock) with respect to ISOs and NQOs. These include a so-called "six-month rule," which requires such individuals to forfeit profits realized through the purchase and sale of the company's stock within that period of time.

Chapter 9

Who's in charge here?

79. Delegating the workload

PROBLEM: There's just too much to be done and too little time to do it in. If you get sick for a day or two, it takes two weeks of late nights just to get back on track. Admittedly, you find it hard to delegate responsibility. You simply don't think other people can do the kind of job that you can do.

DIAGNOSIS: From the day you go into business, you begin to give it away, piece by piece. Unfortunately, the thing that's usually the hardest to part with is the responsibility, but it's absolutely essential if you expect your business to grow.

Learn to let others share your load. That's what they're paid for. That's how they learn and grow. That's how your organization grows. And that's how you can begin to get some much-needed relief.

Franchise businesses have taken the country by storm over the past three decades. Why? Because they begin with the best thinking of numerous experts, combine it, condense it, create a formula from it and then pass it along to a host of other people—their franchisees. If Ray Kroc had not been willing to relinquish a little control and share some of his knowledge with other people, McDonalds probably would still be operating a one-location hamburger stand today.

Those who fail to delegate often get so involved in details that they can no longer see the forest for the trees. They soon discover that their inability to handle the heavy workload is beginning to restrict their growth. Other adverse effects:

- It makes a company too dependent on a single individual and a single point of view.
- Subordinates tend to fall victim to "group-think."

- Limiting the growth potential of your employees, both professionally and economically, causes internal dissatisfaction and often results in the loss of key personnel.
- By limiting growth, it may open the door for new competition.

PRESCRIPTION: Take a stab at creating an organization chart.

Put your own name at the top. You are the boss, and delegating some of the workload is not going to change that. You are—and always will be, as long as you are the head of the company—the final authority on everything.

Below your name, list the most capable, most trusted of your employees (there may be two, three, four or more of them, depending on the size of your organization). As a rule of thumb, try to select approximately one "supervisor" for every seven people or so. In a company with 50 employees, that would mean appointing seven supervisors—probably no more and perhaps a few less. These are the people you have selected to be your "lieutenants."

Now make a list of the most important "departments" of your company. The list will include such things as billing and accounting, sales and marketing, manufacturing and warehousing.

Delegate one department to each of your supervisors, assigning each department to the person who is best qualified to handle it by virtue of skill, experience and specialized knowledge. This probably will entail nothing more than giving a title to someone who already has been handling the job.

If some department is small and closely related to another department, perhaps you can assign both departments to one supervisor, but do *not* put someone in charge of a department for which he or she is totally unsuited and unqualified, even if that means creating an accounting department that has only two employees.

Tell these new managers that you are going to begin transferring some of your responsibilities to them. Stress that the transition will be gradual so they can become accustomed to their new duties, and that you will see to it that, if they feel it is needed, they will receive additional supervisory training. Tell them where their authority begins and ends. Assure them that you will not be a Monday morning quarterback, that you are open to suggestions for change if it will benefit the company and that they have your whole-hearted support.

Create a compensation system that not only rewards the supervisors for their increased responsibility, but encourages them to constantly strive to do better.

Set up a reporting system that guarantees you a prompt, meaningful flow of information from each department. Use this as your means of monitoring your supervisors' work, rather than peering over their shoulders constantly. If everything is going well, leave things alone and let the organization work for you.

For the first year or so, hold monthly meetings attended by all of your department heads. Discuss the company's overall goals and how you are progressing toward them. Share information and ideas. Listen to suggestions and complaints.

If problems arise in a particular department, hold separate meetings with that department head weekly—or even daily in severe cases. If the supervisor is unable to resolve the problem within a reasonable period of time or at an acceptable cost, do not hesitate to replace him or her with someone who is more capable.

Above all, be patient. Employees will not be able to adjust to their new responsibilities overnight. Moreover, it takes time for them to accept the fact that you are willing to relinquish some of your authority to them, and for you to respect and trust their capabilities.

78. Setting an example

PROBLEM: You are spending more and more time explaining how you want things done. Then, when your back is turned, your employees do what *they* think is best. Everywhere you look there is inconsistency. You feel frustrated and ineffective.

DIAGNOSIS: You are not setting the right example by being an ineffective leader.

PRESCRIPTION: Everyone needs a good example to follow. You must provide it by being a strong, focused leader and by instituting solid, sensible operating procedures. Your personal example will always be important, because employees will learn to favor the behavior you favor.

To be a good leader, you must:

- ➲ **Develop a vision.** People want to follow someone who knows where he or she is going.
- ➲ **Become an expert.** People want to understand that you know what you're talking about.
- ➲ **Act as a guide.** Envision the big picture, simplify it, communicate it to your employees and see that your company does not stray from the path leading toward the goals you've set forth.

- **Invite dissent.** People won't give you their best effort or become leaders themselves if they're afraid to speak up and voice an opposing point of view.

- **Encourage risk.** If the employees feel that any slight failure might endanger their careers, they're not likely to suggest progressive new ideas—the kind of ideas that may give you a badly needed edge over your competition.

- **Control your disposition.** Do not overreact to the highs and lows that are to be expected in the normal course of doing business. For the most part, successful businesses run on an even keel, and good leaders strive to keep it that way. Too much time, energy and money are wasted when a company begins to pursue one thing after another in an attempt to respond to some perceived danger.

- **Trust your subordinates.** You rely on each other, but they won't give you their best efforts unless they feel that you believe in them enough to place your trust in them.

79. Controls are vital

PROBLEM: When the business was small, you could keep an eye on things by checking the cash register tapes at the end of the day and balancing the checkbook at the end of the month. Now, with three dozen employees, 20 suppliers, hundreds of customers and annual sales running in six figures, it's hard to stay on top of it all.

DIAGNOSIS: Somewhere along the way, you neglected to set up the right kind of controls—systems and procedures that measure your progress and let you monitor how well the business is operating at the same time.

PRESCRIPTION: Businesses may vary according to their size, the industry, the market, the economy and a number of other factors. But it is essential for a successful CEO to keep his or her eye on some key business indicators:

Sales

- Daily, check total sales.
- Weekly, check the sales of three or four of your major product divisions.
- Monthly, review sales by geographical region and each major product category.
- Occasionally, check sales to top customers.

Ratio of gross profit to net sales

- Making a sale is not the same as making a profit.
- Weekly, look at gross profit ratios for the total business, for each major product category and for 10 or 15 of the major individual items.

Direct expenses

- Large discretionary items such as travel and entertainment should be checked carefully.
- Review any expense item over $3,000.
- Insist on a breakdown of all items listed as "other" if they amount to $100 or more.
- Monthly, review *all* areas of the company.

Other income and expense

- This can cover interest payments, currency exchange gains and losses, and a number of other unusual items. Weekly, look over this miscellaneous category.

Net profit

- Check monthly.

Cash flow

- Weekly, monitor this situation to be sure there's enough cash on hand to pay your suppliers.

Accounts receivable

- It's easy to let these accounts mount up. You want total current accounts to increase in proportion to overdue accounts and the average days outstanding to stay in line.
- Examine the schedule monthly.

Inventory

- Weekly and monthly, check inventory levels against projections of how much inventory will be needed to support average estimated sales.
- How fast can you get material if you begin to run out? Are costs rising or falling?
- Be sure your inventory is current and sellable.

Research and development

- ➲ Monthly, monitor R&D activity.
- ➲ Compare the cost of each project to its projected gross profit.
- ➲ Do all continuing projects still fit into your plans and are they still based on reasonable assumptions?
- ➲ Tell the managers responsible for each of these areas what you are monitoring and that you will expect a detailed explanation, within 24 to 48 hours, if you find any variances from the company's objectives.

Unless you see some warning signals in one or more of the areas outlined here, don't interfere with the company's day-to-day operations.

80. How to use outside advisers

PROBLEM: You're not happy with the answers and recommendations of your key people and wonder if you should consult with someone outside the company who can be more objective. Most often, this requires a person who has had special training or experience in a specialized field, such as banking, accounting or law.

You may find it hard to deal with these people, however. They sometimes speak a different language. You are never sure that you are talking to the most qualified person. And you may have the feeling that they are more interested in their fee than in helping you solve your problem.

How can you feel more secure about engaging an adviser and following their advice?

DIAGNOSIS: There is no doubt that an adviser will look at your situation in a different way than you do. That is one of the reasons you have engaged him or her—to study your problem from a different viewpoint.

PRESCRIPTION: Always seek advice from those inside the company first. Your employees usually are more aware of the unique circumstances associated with your problem, and have the greatest stake in finding a workable solution to it. They also are less likely to resist any change required to implement the solution if they have had a hand in recommending it.

Having said that, we recognize that it is sometimes wise to engage an outsider to review the recommendations of an employee, just to make sure that they are complete and well-founded.

If an outsider must be engaged, the best choice is one who—although not connected with your company—is familiar with your business or industry and has had experience in dealing with similar problems. Such an adviser should be both knowledgeable and up-to-date on industry trends. Further, you must be absolutely sure that you can rely on his or her discretion when it comes to guarding your company secrets.

As you would have had an outsider review the recommendations of an employee, it also is wise to have key employees review the recommendations of an outsider to see that they are suitable, applicable and practical when applied to your unique situation.

Realize that outside advisers come with their own sets of biases. Those who are accustomed to dealing with large corporations may not be able to downscale their thinking to meet your needs. Some technically advanced individuals may tend to advocate "blue sky" solutions, and be too quick to recommend state-of-the-art changes that could be both premature and costly.

Remember that it is the adviser who is paid to make recommendations, not to implement them. It is up to *you* to determine whether the adviser's recommendations are worth pursuing.

81. How to learn from your banker

PROBLEM: You discover that you have reached your borrowing limit at your bank and you don't know where to turn. A friend tells you he got a lot of good advice from his banker.

DIAGNOSIS: It's to your banker's advantage to share what he or she knows with you—if you'll only ask. Some banks actively recruit small business accounts. Some sponsor small business workshops or seminars.

PRESCRIPTION: When you need help in the following areas, don't hesitate to ask your banker:

- ➲ Whether your business plan makes sense.
- ➲ Whether your cash-flow projections are realistic.
- ➲ Which accountants, lawyers and other business professionals could be of help to you.

- Advice on the outlook for development in your community, as well as for the business climate in general.
- Where to look for potential clients.
- What you can do to make your business most attractive when you need a loan.

To get the most value from your relationship with a banker:

- Think of your banker as a member of your management team.
- Talk to your banker about your business and see whether he or she has any suggestions to make.
- Have your banker review your business plan and visit your business occasionally to see what you do and how you do it.
- Inform your banker of what is going on in your business, even if it's bad news.

82. Learning from your accountant

PROBLEM: You want to acquire a competitor. In the due diligence process their accounting firm raises many difficult questions about your financial records.

DIAGNOSIS: Good accounting is absolutely essential for any business. In addition, a solid relationship can bring many more benefits beyond accurate financial and tax records.

PRESCRIPTION: Consult your accountant when you need help on such matters as these:

- Advice on updating your record-keeping system.
- Help in selecting or training bookkeeping staff.
- Keeping track of your income, payroll, accounts receivable and payable and other types of expense.
- Help in developing your business plan.
- Advice on how to find outside financing.
- Preparing financial statements when you are applying for a loan.
- Preparing regular reports, including profit and loss statements.

- Preparing special reports, such as a break-even analysis, a year-at-a-glance comparison, tax-consequence evaluations, feasibility studies and cost-reduction evaluations.
- Recommendations regarding long-term business investments and tax strategies.
- Along with legal advisers, drawing up contracts, leases and other documents.
- Recommendations regarding bankers and attorneys who specialize in working with small businesses.

83. Do you have the right lawyer?

PROBLEM: You are surprised to learn that your company has had two law suits filed against it in the past six weeks—one by a disgruntled former employee for age discrimination and the other by a new vendor for breach of contract.

DIAGNOSIS: You must have access to a compatible attorney and competent legal advice *before* a crisis arises.

PRESCRIPTION: Here are some ways to maximize benefits from your relationship with an attorney:

- Check out the attorney's reputation and expertise with other clients.
- See if the attorney offers an initial consultation free of charge.
- See how well-organized the attorney seems to be.
- See if the attorney keeps you waiting.
- See how quickly the attorney responds to a telephone call.
- See if the attorney bills you for every brief conversation or only for actual conference sessions.

84. Getting more from your advisers

PROBLEM: You turned to a couple of outside advisers when you were not satisfied with employees answers. Now you are worried that the outsiders' recommendations are not trustworthy.

DIAGNOSIS: It does little good to look for outside advice if you don't pay any attention to it or won't act upon it.

PRESCRIPTION: To get the most out of your conferences with an outside adviser:

- Teach your adviser about your business by providing him or her with brochures, newsletters, magazines, price lists, advertisements and so on. The more your adviser knows about your business, the better he or she can help you.

- Give your adviser advance notice about important situations.

- Batch your questions instead of taking them one at a time.

- If you don't understand an adviser's suggestion, ask for further explanation.

- If you do not plan to follow your adviser's advice, explain why.

- If you consistently don't like your adviser's suggestions, find another adviser.

85. No substitute for personal contact

PROBLEM: Early on, you knew every employee in the company and it was possible to maintain a personal relationship with each one of them. Now that the company has grown, that firsthand intimacy is no longer practical, and you're afraid that you may be losing touch with many of your best workers.

DIAGNOSIS: Contact with employees at all levels of the company helps you to keep tabs on what's going on throughout the business. It also helps you spot rising new talent.

PRESCRIPTION: An approach that works for some executives is to schedule appointments every four months with the middle managers *who do not report directly to them*. In that way, they can ask questions not only about their employees' individual—often critical—areas of responsibility, but about matters involving operations one step above and one step below. This gives you an opportunity to answer such questions as:

➲ Do your managers give you all of the support that you need?

➲ Are your managers willing to listen to your suggestions for improvement?

➲ Are your managers encouraging the people who report to them to recommend ways of doing their work better, faster, cheaper or more efficiently?

➲ If your managers were asked to grade the efficiency of their units, what grade would they give? Why? What are some ways to raise the grade?

86. Mentoring

PROBLEM: Unable to keep track of every individual in the company, you rely on your key managers to bring outstanding performers to your attention. Unfortunately, such people tend to become disenchanted and anxious to move on to other opportunities if they feel that their talents aren't being appreciated.

DIAGNOSIS: You might consider adopting the practice of mentoring—that is, using your top personnel as special counselors to the younger ones.

PRESCRIPTION: Mentoring is seldom successful unless the program is *totally* voluntary. Some seniors tend to view juniors as competitors, threats to their positions and their authority. A senior should never be coerced into acting as a mentor, nor should a junior be coerced into accepting a mentor.

Whenever both parties enter into the relationship voluntarily, however, the results can be extremely rewarding.

A good mentor should:

➩ Never counsel a direct subordinate. It is not possible to act as both a supervisor and a counselor.

➩ Never be dogmatic or dictatorial.

➩ Always encourage a free exchange of ideas and opinions.

➩ Guarantee the person counseled complete confidentiality.

➩ Listen to the individual's problems, but offer advice only when asked to.

➩ Involve the individual in as many meetings as possible involving corporate and customer policy.

87. When a partner wants out

PROBLEM: After many years together, your partner has announced that he would like to retire. You would like to continue in the business, but you can't afford to buy out your partner's share of the company.

DIAGNOSIS: An exit system should be built into every partnership agreement at the very beginning. "Golden handshakes" seldom work when it comes time to exercise them.

When one partner suddenly wants out of the business, it often comes at a bad time for the remaining partner. Animosity often results, along with awkwardness, delays, confusion, a gap in the division of responsibilities and a variety of other complications that may even reach out into the company's relationships with customers and suppliers.

PRESCRIPTION: Dissolution of a business is one of the strongest arguments in favor of turning the company into a corporation at the earliest possible opportunity. True, there are other advantages to incorporation as well:

- ➲ Security—sheltering your personal assets from lawsuits incurred by the business.

- ➲ The ability to increase the owners' investment—and hence the value—of the business whenever necessary, either by buying more stock yourself or by selling shares to outsiders, including key employees.

But the ability to more readily value and vend a partner's share in the business at the time he or she wishes to leave it is one of the most valuable. It is one means of assuring that the company will go on, even if one or more of the principles has left.

One way of dealing with this situation, for example, would be to devise an exit system that calls for a partner to be properly "vested" in the company at the time he or she decides to leave it. The individual's shares could be vested at, say, five, six or even 10 years, as predetermined when the system is established.

Shares in the company can be valued as they might be if they were being sold on the open stock market. Once the partner's interest is vested, he or she can deal with the shares as if they were cash—taking them to the company financial officer and putting them in at "market rates."

Each shareholder would have the option of selling as many shares as he or she wishes—from one share to his or her entire holdings—whenever it's necessary. The shares so offered might be purchased by the company itself or by any other individual who has been authorized to do so. If the remaining principle in the business does not wish to buy out the partner and/or the company is not in a financial position to buy the shares, they could be offered to valued employees, loyal customers, vendors or others who are deemed to be of value as part-owners of the business.

Whatever device is established, a workable exit system should be included as a part of all business partnerships.

88. Choosing your successor

PROBLEM: Now that the business is running smoothly—and you have reached the age where it seems appealing to live a quieter life—you are beginning to think of stepping aside to make room for someone else who can run the company on a day-to-day basis.

DIAGNOSIS: If it was difficult to learn to delegate responsibility to other people, it will be doubly difficult to turn over the company reins to someone else—but it is important to formulate a plan for leaving the business and to do so as early in the game as possible. It gives you and your potential successors something to strive for and it spells out the parameters by which it will be accomplished.

Having a plan for exiting the company keeps you honest. It forces you to test the value of what you are doing. But selecting the right successor may not be an easy task.

PRESCRIPTION: If the prospects for the future are good and new ventures are likely, you should find someone who will:

- Keep employees satisfied and happy.
- Stimulate new ideas.
- Start new projects.
- Maximize shareholder value.

If the prospects are not so good, however, you probably should look for a person who:

- Will operate a "lean and mean" company.
- Minimize risk.
- Concentrate on a critical few projects.
- Control costs and focus resources.

Chapter 10

When hard work is wasted

91. Serving *and* controlling

PROBLEM: You have staffed your company well and everyone demonstrates a strong work ethic, but it often seems like you're riding off in all directions at once. Administration does its work, marketing does its work and product planning does its work, but each one sometimes acts like the other components of the company don't even exist.

DIAGNOSIS: Most employees are task-oriented. They know how to do their jobs, but they have little concern about how the other people in the organization do their work or why.

One of the primary duties of the CEO is to bridge this gap by demonstrating to all employees that the company is like a team, detailing what the components of that team are and explaining how each component relates to the others. Employees must learn that nobody can work or succeed in a vacuum, and that the success of the company depends upon everyone working together.

PRESCRIPTION: Once a company has attained a reasonable size, it should have two distinct types of staff: control staff and service staff. (By "staff," we mean employees involved in functions that are not directly related to the production, sale or distribution of your product.)

Control staff handles duties delegated by the CEO, such as:

- Setting personnel policies.
- Establishing purchasing policies.
- Handling the accounting.
- Budgeting.
- Policy-making functions, in general.

Control functions usually are project-oriented and generally are based on the company's objectives. The rationale behind them should be clearly communicated to everyone concerned.

Projects involving control staff should be prioritized according to their contribution to the company's strategic objectives. They should be closely monitored by the CEO to see that they meet their objectives on schedule and within preestablished cost restraints.

Service staff, on the other hand, performs duties that will enable operational managers, such as production managers and sales directors, to concentrate on managing and developing their respective departments. Such duties may include:

- Interviewing job candidates.

- Evaluating software packages.

- Getting cost bids from vendors.

- Task-oriented, rather than policy-making functions, in general.

Projects involving service staff usually are transaction-oriented, and consist of implementing and administering established policies, processes and systems. As a result, it's often best to have these functions decentralized and reporting to the lowest and most closely related level of management. In small companies, however, service staff personnel often share an office.

Both types of staff are engaged to help the company achieve its strategic, competitive and profit goals. Both should be evaluated regularly in order to measure their effectiveness.

Not hiring staff soon enough can slow your growth, put you at a competitive disadvantage and reduce your profits. Hiring staff too soon, not hiring the right people or not using staff personnel wisely can be equally disastrous, however.

There are a number of periodicals on the market that can be invaluable to those who operate small businesses. Some of the best include:

- *Boardroom Reports*
- *Business Horizons*
- *Human Resource Executive*
- *Small Business Reports*
- *The Pryor Report*
- *Success*

- *Bottom Line Personal*
- *Inc.*
- *Entrepreneur*
- *Management Review*
- *Executive Excellence*
- *Communication Briefings*

92. Using time as a resource

PROBLEM: Between managing a staff and answering inquiries from customers, vendors and a variety of other people, you don't seem to get a lot accomplished each day.

Is it possible to squeeze a little more time out of the workday?

DIAGNOSIS: Other than to delegate more of your work, there are a few changes in your personal habits that might give you a little more breathing room.

PRESCRIPTION: To accomplish more during the workday, try the following:

- Do a task immediately. Avoid procrastination.

- Don't avoid unpleasant tasks. They simply pile up, adding to your workload.

- Do the easiest jobs first. The feeling of accomplishment, knowing that these things are out of the way, will stimulate you to tackle the tougher jobs.

- Tackle your work in the order of its importance. That way, the major things will get done and if anything's left over, it won't be anything very important.

- Alternate difficult tasks and easy tasks. The easy work gives you a bit of a breather—a chance to recuperate—at intervals throughout the day.

- Group similar tasks. That way, you only need to get out the materials that you need one time, rather than three or four.

- Change tasks every couple of hours. Staying with one thing for too long becomes boring, uninspiring, stale. Something new will clear your mind so that you can work better when you go back to your original task.

93. Resolving internal tensions

PROBLEM: You have been having a succession of problems involving differences between your marketing division and your manufacturing division. Is this necessary?

DIAGNOSIS: Necessary, no—but not uncommon. Many companies experience difficulties between these two departments.

PRESCRIPTION: Marketing decides what products to offer and in what variety. Manufacturing decides how to produce the most profitable quantities of those products.

Greater variety permits the company to tailor its products more closely to the needs of the market and either charge more for those products or sell more units. There are offsetting costs, however, including the need to maintain larger inventories.

There is an optimum combination that will produce the most profits for the firm. The marketing manager and the manufacturing manager, on their own, may not have enough information to reach that decision.

The solution: Insist that they work together and bring you a solution that will work for the company as a whole. Each will usually have to compromise.

94. The cure for too many meetings

PROBLEM: A steady schedule of meetings eats up nearly all of your time. While it's necessary to meet with your staff to communicate important information and gather data and feedback, it seems no one is getting anything else done.

DIAGNOSIS: You seem to be letting your meetings run you, rather than seeing to it that you run your meetings.

PRESCRIPTION: Not all meetings are bad. Indeed, well-planned meetings, attended by the appropriate participants and held to an intelligent agenda, can be very beneficial.

Meetings can:

- Improve the downward flow of information.
- Promote the upward flow of information.
- Aid in decision-making.
- Help to implement change.
- Help to develop a team spirit.

Generally speaking, there are three kinds of meetings: *problem-solving* and *planning meetings*, best held to about six participants; *training meetings*, best limited to 20 to 30 participants; and *informational meetings*, capable of accommodating as many as can be comfortably seated.

In addition, *ad hoc meetings* are often useful for discussing highly important issues and resolving immediate questions. They should always by kept short and to the point.

Of course, some companies tend to hold entirely too many meetings, and that tendency should be avoided at all costs. As an alternate to a meeting, try substituting:

- Telephone conversations.
- One-on-one visits.
- Memos.

95. Meeting preparation

PROBLEM: Typically, half of the time allotted for a meeting is wasted before participants focus on the real issue.

DIAGNOSIS: This situation is easily eliminated by better preparation *before* the meeting.

PRESCRIPTION: These planning pointers can help to improve the focus of your meetings considerably:

➲ Involve invitees in preparing the agenda for the meeting. Ask them for:

- Suggested topics for discussion.
- Time limitations for the meeting.
- Supporting documents to be used at the meeting.
- A list of who should be invited to the meeting.

➲ Allow the participants to prepare and gather any necessary documentation by distributing an agenda *in advance* of the meeting. Be sure it includes:

- Date, time and location of the meeting.
- Order of business.
- Time allotted to each item.
- What is to be accomplished.
- Questions and issues that are likely to arise.
- What information, documentation or other materials the participants should take to the meeting.

➲ If time allows after the agenda has been covered, you can open the meeting to discussion. This allows participants to air their concerns and feel that their ideas and problems are important.

96. Who should attend?

PROBLEM: Almost every time you hold a meeting, you discover that there are participants who don't belong there and others who, had they been there, would have been beneficial to the discussions.

DIAGNOSIS: Too often, meetings involve a preset list of participants, rather than a list that has been created specifically for that meeting.

PRESCRIPTION: Instead of automatically inviting a set group of individuals to your meetings, invite only those who are involved in the matters to be discussed.

In addition, those who are invited to attend your meetings should:

➲ Have the authority to make and carry out decisions.

➲ Have knowledge regarding the issue(s) under discussion.

➲ Be able to provide or need to receive information.

97. Handling cynics and silent types

PROBLEM: Some participants are habitually negative about everything under discussion. Others never talk during the meeting, but "bad mouth" all decisions later.

DIAGNOSIS: This will happen for as long as you allow it to happen.

PRESCRIPTION: Try to preempt the grousers by stating at the outset that you are aware of opposing views (and don't need to hear repetitions of them at the meeting). You may also meet with such people in advance of the meeting, give them an opportunity to state their point of view and conclude by making it clear that you would like them to keep an open mind and attend the meeting without hostility.

Other participants may be loathe to contribute to the discussion. You may be able to draw them out by:

• Establishing eye contact with them.

• Addressing them by name.

• Asking them open-ended questions.

• Requesting that all participants write down their ideas regarding the topic under discussion.

98. Increasing participation

PROBLEM: Too often, the participants in your meetings simply sit there, unprepared and seemingly bored to death. Is there some way to wake them up?

DIAGNOSIS: Visuals can be useful and they improve the participants' retention. Without visuals, studies show people will retain only 10 percent; with visuals, approximately 50 percent.

PRESCRIPTION: Other ways to improve the productivity of your meetings might include:

- Encouraging disagreement. Constructive criticism and debate (but not uncontrolled argument) can be highly effective.

- Do not let an individual dominate the meeting. It wastes time and discourages others from making a contribution.

- If it will be a long meeting, allow for an occasional break.

- Avoid making a decision when the disagreements on the subject have become heated. Move on to another topic instead, with plans to return to the controversial subject later.

- If no opposing view is forthcoming, play devil's advocate to stimulate free thinking and discussion.

- Use the last five minutes of the meeting to summarize the highlights of the discussion and the decisions that were reached. Repeat all assignments and deadlines that were agreed upon.

- Conclude your meetings on time and on a positive note.

99. Follow-up

PROBLEM: When participants leave your meetings, they have surprisingly little retention of what happened there. Can that situation be improved upon?

DIAGNOSIS: You are tempted to conclude that (a) the material covered in the meeting was not pertinent to the participants, or (b) it was so poorly presented that they failed to see how it applied to them.

Unfortunately, studies clearly demonstrate that participants simply do not retain as much information as they should.

PRESCRIPTION: Participants' retention can be augmented by distributing an in-depth minutes within 24 hours of the meeting. With the minutes, distribute an evaluation questionnaire that asks:

- ➲ Was the meeting necessary?
- ➲ Was an agenda distributed?
- ➲ Did the participants help formulate the agenda?
- ➲ Were supporting documents distributed with the agenda?
- ➲ Was the agenda followed during the meeting?
- ➲ Were the desired results achieved?
- ➲ Was the time of the meeting convenient?
- ➲ Did the meeting begin and end on time?
- ➲ Were the facilities satisfactory?
- ➲ Were the goals of the meeting clearly defined?
- ➲ Did the topics on the agenda result in conclusions and decisions?
- ➲ Was action assigned?
- ➲ Were priorities set?
- ➲ Were all attendees involved in the discussion?
- ➲ Was order maintained and were proper procedures followed?
- ➲ Were accurate records and minutes kept?
- ➲ Are follow-up procedures being observed?
- ➲ Were the participants satisfied with the way in which the meeting was conducted?

Chapter 11

Handling finances

100. Maintaining financial control

PROBLEM: For the past three months you have been surprised at month's end to discover that profits were much lower than expected.

DIAGNOSIS: Financial control can make the difference between making a profit, breaking even or going down the tubes.

PRESCRIPTION: There are several areas to keep your eye on simultaneously:

- ➲ Keep a close eye on the bills.
  - Take advantage of volume discounts.
  - Earn discounts and/or avoid late charges by paying your bills promptly.
  - Always be on the alert for less-expensive sources of supply *as long as they don't entail a cut in quality.*
- ➲ Keep an equally close eye on the receivables.
  - Money in the till is better than money on the books.
  - Don't hurt yourself by financing other people.
- ➲ Watch your inventories.
  - If you carry stock that isn't moving, it's costing you money.
  - The faster your inventory turns over, the better.
- ➲ Be realistic about your facilities, equipment and employment.
  - Don't waste money on a fancy address that you don't need.
  - Don't waste money on a larger facility than you need.
  - Don't invest in equipment that is larger or more complex than you need.
  - Don't carry people on the payroll that aren't earning their keep.

101. Causes of unnecessary costs

PROBLEM: Your efforts to cut costs have been ineffective so far. While you've managed to reduce some expenditures, your budget cuts have had detrimental effects on productivity or quality. You just can't seem to identify what expenses are unnecessary.

DIAGNOSIS: Many cost-cutting efforts fail because they effect "things," rather than causes. Cuts are made, but the company's basic cost structure remains the same. The cost-cutting did not alter or improve the company's work processes in the least.

Example: The company lays off a large number of people, but it does not change the way in which it is handling its work. As a result:

- The same amount of work needs to be done, therefore the department heads have to hire temporaries or independent contractors to do it—often at a higher hourly rate than the original employees had been paid.

- Since the same amount of work has to be done, there are now holes in the operation, causing mistakes to occur, waste levels to rise, rejection rates to increase and quality to suffer.

PRESCRIPTION: Rather than use simple across-the-board methods of cost-cutting, employ the principles of cost management:

➲ **Develop and use meaningful cost information.**

- Issue a weekly report that shows each manager the status of costs over which he or she has direct control. Working with timely data, the manager can more effectively control expenses.

- Be sure the other employees know of your efforts to control costs and also are made a part of the process.

➲ **Simplify your work processes by eliminating waste, complexity and bureaucracy.**

- Remove unnecessary approvals.

- Do away with unneeded reports.

- If there is a step in the process that fails to add value to what you produce, remove it.

- Avoid all forms of work duplication.

➲ **Link each employee's contribution to compensation.**
- See that employees receive the proper training.
- Make sure employees understand your system(s).
- Encourage employees to seek better ways to do their work.
- Encourage supervisors to respond to workers' cost-cutting recommendations.

102. Is your product priced too low?

PROBLEM: Your sales volume is good, but your net profit is disappointing. Your prices have been the same for 12 months.

DIAGNOSIS: Look carefully at both pricing and costs.

PRESCRIPTION: How do your prices compare with those of your competitors? If you are greatly underpriced, you may be enjoying a nice sales volume but hurting your profit margin.

Raise your prices moderately or, better yet, see if you can't get a better price for your product by enhancing the quality ("new and improved") or quantity ("now 10 percent bigger").

Also see if you can't lower your costs by such means as:

➲ Buying bulk quantities.

➲ Reducing the size of your sales force.

➲ Adjusting your promotional budget.

103. Evaluating your cash flow

PROBLEM: Business is growing, new clients are coming on board every day and orders are increasing. Things couldn't be better, right? Wrong. Because of increased activity, your expenses are increasing—but the money isn't coming in as fast. Your company is experiencing problems with its cash flow.

DIAGNOSIS: Your company's accounts payable strategy should be based on its own cash-flow requirements. Otherwise, you are, in effect, bankrolling your customers.

PRESCRIPTION: If it takes 120 days to collect on your accounts receivable, it is financially unreasonable for you to pay your own bills within 15 days. Review your cash-flow cycle (that is, the time that elapses from when you spend your money on raw materials, labor, shipping and so forth, through the sales and marketing process, until the time you are paid by your customers).

For the purpose of illustration, assume you are a distributor. You buy a product on February 1, sell it on April 30 and receive payment for it on June 15. In other words, you have had your money "invested" in that product for about 105 days!

If you paid your supplier for the product within 30 days of the time you bought it, you have been "financing" the product for about 75 days!

Remember that your profit is based on how much you mark up your products, and does not include "interest" on whatever money you may have tied up in the product between the time you buy it and the time you sell it. That expense comes directly out of your gross profit.

Focus on these three ways to reduce this cash-to-cash cycle.

- ➲ Collect money from your customers faster.
- ➲ Move your product faster.
- ➲ Pay your own bills slower.

104. Managing accounts payable

PROBLEM: Your accountant tells you that the company is experiencing cash-flow problems due to the lenient handling of accounts payable.

DIAGNOSIS: Reconsider your accounts payable policies and make any necessary adjustments. Avoid putting an accounting clerk in the position of having to decide which bills are to be paid and when.

PRESCRIPTION: Begin by evaluating your cash-flow position and determining your needs. Then set collection goals that will permit you to coordinate the receipt of incoming cash with the need for outgoing cash.

Date checks no earlier than the dates on which the payments are due. Try to hold on to your cash as long as possible and still maintain a good credit rating with your suppliers.

Establish a two-tiered list of payment priorities:

1. The group that should be paid at all costs and on whatever terms have been agreed upon.
   - Major vendors.
   - Service suppliers.
   - Bankers.
   - Local, state and federal tax authorities.

2. Minor suppliers whose goodwill is less important to the welfare of your company.

Be sure your accounting department knows about these payment priorities—and which companies fall into which categories.

Dealing with those you owe

An important part of doing business successfully involves your ability to negotiate. Whenever you deal with a supplier—or a customer—try to negotiate the most favorable terms possible *for yourself.* You can be assured that the other party is doing the same.

With respect to your accounts payable, you have some leverage you can use to negotiate better-than-usual terms with your major suppliers, especially when business is slow. The best time to negotiate is when the order is being placed, not when payment is due.

Maintaining good records

You should have good accounts payable records, including weekly updates on the aging of every outstanding bill. Interest charges for financing late payables can become expensive.

Distribute a payables "problems list" each month to all of your managers so everyone will know what the potential trouble spots are.

105. How to avoid fraud in payables

PROBLEM: You have discovered that some employees have been looting your accounts payable. A new employee found that health insurance premiums had been underpaid and several vendor invoices had been altered.

DIAGNOSIS: Unscrupulous individuals who have access to company checks may find it tempting—and surprisingly easy—to pay themselves a little unauthorized bonus. Unfortunately, this is a fairly common form of employee theft. But guard against it by following these steps:

PRESCRIPTION: Formalize your payment procedures in such a way as to provide a double check at each step of the process.

- Bills should be paid only when they have been matched with a purchase order and a delivery confirmation.
- One person should be assigned to write or authorize checks, but another person should be authorized to sign them.

- Blank checks should be kept under lock-and-key.
- All check numbers, including voided checks, should be tracked regularly.
- Be sure the checkbook balances each month.
- If a computerized payment system is involved, access should be denied to everyone except by the approved computer code.
- If a payment is made by wire transfer, bank procedures should be established to guarantee proper control.

106. Dealing with a cash crisis

PROBLEM: Cash is scarce, outside sources of funding have dried up, internal sources of funding are inadequate to cover your needs, existing lenders are becoming nervous and credit agreements are coming close to default.

Employees are frightened and suppliers are worried that they won't get paid. Members of your board of directors are looking for a good reason to resign.

DIAGNOSIS: You need to take control of your cash—fast! Find it, protect it, enhance it and control the flow.

PRESCRIPTION: Take personal charge of the cash. Uncover any pools of it that haven't been tapped and look for ways of stretching the dollar as much as possible:

- Shorten the terms of payment for your customers, especially:
  - Foreign customers.
  - Favored customers with "sweet" terms.
- With suppliers, *lengthen* your terms of payment as much as possible.
- Look for other sources of cash:
  - Sell worthwhile but nonessential assets.
  - Drop frills, such as first-class travel and club memberships.
- Monitor your cash position continuously and know how much cash is on hand at all times.

Now that you have bought some time by taking control of the company's cash, try to find out where there are profit-reducing "leaks":

- Weed out all cash-consuming, nonessential operations.
- Involve employees who can help you straighten things out.

⮩ Identify as many curable problems as possible, patch them up as well as you can and initiate programs that will produce permanent remedies.

⮩ Go after the three or four biggest cash-drains and attack them mercilessly.

⮩ Keep your eyes open for new opportunities. Think in terms of cash...cash...*cash*. Select a few projects and put your full resources to work.

⮩ Create a short-term plan:

 • Begin by looking 90 days ahead.

 • Gradually, move your target farther and farther out.

 • Raise new cash.

 • Using your new plan(s), see if you can't locate some new sources of capital and retap some of the old sources.

⮩ Reestablish credibility:

 • Meet your responsibilities as stated.

 • Establish yourself as someone who has accomplished a turnaround.

⮩ Improve everybody's attitude:

 • Project the company as a survivor to employees, stock-holders, suppliers, customers, lenders and the media.

107. Staying on top of inventory

PROBLEM: Your inventory is out of control. Your last physical inventory count was off by 15 percent and your book orders are the highest ever.

DIAGNOSIS: You can set up financial reporting systems that tracks trends in five different kinds of relationships within the company. These systems function as an early-warning system against possible inventory problems.

PRESCRIPTION: Implement the following systems and follow them carefully as a safeguard against future inventory problems:

1. Gross margin return on investment

Subtract the cost of your product's raw materials, direct labor and factory overhead, including your warehousing costs from your selling price. Then divide that by the selling price. Leave out administrative costs should be left out.

➲ A manufacturer should be able to demonstrate a 15 to 25 percent return on each product line.

➲ A distributor who has no production expenses simply subtracts the cost of goods *bought* from goods *sold* and divides that by his selling price. The goal should be a 25 percent rate of return.

➲ Some practical ways to improve your profit picture:

  • If even your bestselling lines are not profitable, eliminate them.

  • Look for ways to reduce costs in all lines.

Example: Instead of offering your customers packages in a dozen shades of red, all of which will have to be stocked in inventory, reduce their choices to two. (Side benefit: Since customers are now in a position to buy the two colors in larger quantities, they can get a better price.)

2. Inventory turnover

A good inventory-tracking system will tell you how often every product in inventory is used and replaced. The inventory should turn over as often as possible to minimize the amount of cash you have tied up in the warehouse.

➲ To determine the rate of turnover by product, divide the total number of units sold during the year by the average number of units on hand during the year.

  As a rule, a manufacturer's inventory should turn over six to eight times a year. If it only turns over three times a year, you have tied up twice as much cash in warehousing as necessary. The cost: whatever interest that money could have earned if it were in an investment account.

  This is not to say that you shouldn't stock up on raw materials if you can find a particularly good deal, but you have to be sure your cost savings outweighs the additional expense of supporting a slow inventory turnover. (These costs are the price of warehouse overhead, including labor, plus the interest that was lost on the money that was tied up in inventory.)

➲ Track finished and online goods weekly, and raw materials monthly.

3. Percentage of orders shipped on time

If the inventory turns over too quickly, lean companies may not be able to fill their orders as promptly as they should. To make sure you don't overmanage your inventory:

➲ Keep track of the percentage of orders that are shipped on time.

➲ Try to fill orders according to the delivery terms you have set up with your customers 98 percent of the time.

➲ Monitor this ratio on a product-by-product basis once or twice a month. If the percentage of on-time shipments drops below the mid-90s, you probably need to pump up your inventory levels.

4. Time it takes to fill back orders

➲ Monitor on a weekly basis how long it takes to fill back orders.

➲ If you know you're going to sell 50 items a week and you know that it takes two weeks to make those 50 items, then keep at least 100 of them in stock.

➲ If you see your orders increase to 70 items per week, react immediately by increasing your production enough to keep your inventory in balance with the increased demand.

5. Percentage of customer complaints to shipped orders

➲ Divide the number of customer complaints you receive by the number of orders shipped. If it exceeds 2 percent, you could be facing real problems.

➲ Analyze each complaint to see if you can determine the underlying problem. Example: Incorrectly shipped items might indicate a poor product-tracking system, mislabeled storage bins or badly trained warehouse personnel.

108. Performing a break-even analysis

PROBLEM: Your business plan is based on a profit of 8 percent and you discover that for the quarter to date, you are not even close. Worst of all, you are not certain if you are including all of the necessary variables.

DIAGNOSIS: Perform a break-even analysis of the business. Essentially, this is just a way of determining when your business has reached the break-even point. Only after you've done that can you get on the road to profitability.

PRESCRIPTION: Performing a break-even analysis depends on whether you are in the business of selling a product or a service.

When you sell a product:

- ➲ Determine what items are your fixed costs. These cost the same regardless of your sales volume.
  - Rent.
  - Salaries.
  - Utilities.
  - Interest on loans.
  - Depreciation on machines and equipment.
- ➲ Identify your variable costs. These are the ones you incur specifically to make, buy and sell your product.
  - Materials.
  - Direct labor.
  - Manufacturing overhead.
  - Sales commissions.
- ➲ Add in the items that don't seem to be either "fixed" or "variable," such as advertising.
- ➲ Total these three categories of cost.
- ➲ Subtract your variable costs from your sales total to determine your contribution margin percentage.

Your total fixed costs, divided by the contribution margin percentage, give you your sales break-even point *in dollars*.

To get your sales break-even point *in products*, divide the contribution margin by your total number of units produced. Then divide your total fixed costs by the contribution margin *per unit*.

When you sell a service:

- ➲ Perform the first four steps above.
- ➲ Divide your total income by your total expenses. If your income exceeds your expenses, you are profitable.

109. A workable billing procedure

PROBLEM: Your present billing procedure is far too lax, resulting in frequent problems with the customers.

DIAGNOSIS: Perhaps the following procedures will help you correct the situation.

PRESCRIPTION: Begin the process with a written estimate. Use it as a means of reiterating the description of the goods or services that the customer has requested. In this way, both you and the customer are in agreement as to what you are selling and what he or she is buying. Include:

- ➲ The estimated date of delivery or service.
- ➲ The terms of payment.

Ask the customer to return a signed copy of the estimate to you by a specific date. In some cases, a purchase order may serve the same purpose.

Charge a deposit

Getting a deposit from the customer will improve your cash flow and discourage your customer from shopping around elsewhere. Make clear under what terms the deposit is refundable—if at all.

Present a proper bill

Be sure your bill includes:

- ➲ Your business name, address and telephone number.
- ➲ Your customer's name and address.
- ➲ The date the bill is prepared.
- ➲ The date of the work performed or the item purchased.
- ➲ The nature of the work performed or the item purchased.
- ➲ The amount charged for each service or item purchased.
- ➲ The total amount due, including any taxes and subtracting any deposits or other forms of payment received.
- ➲ A message indicating when you expect to be paid, such as "Due within 30 days of billing date."
- ➲ A statement as to any penalty for late payment.

Subsequent collection efforts

If subsequent bills are sent out, be sure to include:

- ➲ A note marking the bill "Late" or "Past due."
- ➲ The date the bill is prepared.
- ➲ If a third bill is required, specify when payment is expected and what you propose to do if it is not.
- ➲ If you are unable to collect the bill, hire a collection agency. But be aware that a service will charge you anywhere from one-third to one-half of the amount they collect.

110. A budget you can live with

PROBLEM: You try to have a good budget, but it's never realistic. You're always way off in some categories.

DIAGNOSIS: A budget is only as good as the information you use when you prepare it.

PRESCRIPTION: When you sit down to prepare your budget, be sure you have these records on hand:

- ➲ **Cost journal.** Spreadsheets listing the items you expect to buy. Like a check register, it tracks the costs you incur with vendors and others.
- ➲ **Sales journal.** Tracks sales made and reviews received.
- ➲ **Estimated and actual cost detail sheet.** Add up the monthly sales and subtract the monthly expenses. Each month, compare these figures with the ones that you showed on your projected budget.
- ➲ **Estimated and actual sales detail sheet.** Compare actual sales to estimated sales each month.
- ➲ **Estimated detail sheet.** Subtract estimated costs from estimated sales to get your estimated profit margin. A 20-percent margin is healthy.

Each month, review your cash flow, accounts receivable, accounts payable and market analysis. Make any adjustments that may be necessary to keep them in line with your projections.

111. Controlling staff expenses

PROBLEM: Staff expenses are growing out of control.

DIAGNOSIS: There should be legitimate reasons for sharp or significant increases in staff expenses, such as the introduction of a new product or the installation of new equipment. It is important to know when your expenses are going up and why.

PRESCRIPTION: To control staff expenses, account for each professional and technical function separately and compare the cost to something relevant, such as:

- Marketing expense as a percentage of sales.
- Personnel cost per employee.
- Purchasing cost as a percentage of total purchases.
- Data processing costs as a percentage of total costs.

112. Employee health insurance

PROBLEM: The cost of employee health benefits is increasing steadily, and you can't find a way to control them.

DIAGNOSIS: A number of organizations can provide you with useful information and affordable alternatives to control these costs.

PRESCRIPTION: If you need information, contact: 1) your state Department of Insurance or Department of Consumer Affairs; 2) local chambers of commerce; and 3) your trade association.
Other sources of help include:

- The Health Insurance Association of America, 1025 Connecticut Ave. NW, Washington, DC 20036, (202) 223-7780. It provides information on companies that sell major medical policies to individuals.

- The Robert Wood Johnson Foundation's Health Care for the Uninsured Program, P.O. Box 2316, Princeton, NJ 08543, (609) 452-8701. It has a program aimed at uninsured small businesses, especially those with 10 employees or less.

- Quotesmith Corp., Palatine, IL, (800) 556-9393. It tracks rates, coverages and safety ratings of 350 insurance companies, including Blue Cross/Blue Shield. It will provide 25 comparisons for a fee.

• Wilkinson Benefit Consultants Inc., Towson, MD, (410) 832-7503. It maintains a database on 1,000 health plan options and charges a fee based on the number of people you employ.

113. Establishing trade credit

PROBLEM: A competitor is using something called "trade credit," but you don't understand how it works.

DIAGNOSIS: "Trade credit" simply means that you are provided with a supplier's goods or services but not charged for them for at least 30 days, and the vendor charges no interest during that time.

PRESCRIPTION: The trick is to receive the goods, sell them and collect from your customer *before* you have to pay your vendor. In some cases, the vendor will even give you a discount if you pay your bill before it comes due. A vendor may not allow you to conduct business on credit until you have established a satisfactory payment record, particularly if your company is new.

114. Selling receivables: pro or con?

PROBLEM: In an attempt to improve your cash flow, you are thinking about selling your receivables to a third party.

DIAGNOSIS: Like almost anything else, there are some favorable aspects to this alternative—and some unfavorable ones. It all depends on your individual set of circumstances.

PRESCRIPTION: Commercial companies buy your accounts receivables at a discount rate of from 1 to 15 percent. In most cases, the only accounts with a potential for this approach "factoring" are consumer accounts because of the interest charged on the remaining account balances.

The pros:
- You receive your cash immediately.
- You are relieved of the bookkeeping and collection costs associated with maintaining accounts receivable.

The cons:
- You must be in a business that can withstand a discount on its receivables of 1 to 15 percent and still operate profitably.
- By reducing revenue, you'll reduce net profit as well.

115. Can leasing save money?

PROBLEM: You are spending a lot of money on equipment, but find yourself without enough working capital to handle other expenses.

DIAGNOSIS: Instead of using your cash to buy equipment, let the equipment manufacturer "lend" you money by selling the equipment to you over a period of time. This is a particularly good way to cut startup costs.

PRESCRIPTION: In many cases, a lease offers you the option of buying the equipment from the lessor at the time the lease expires.

There are two common contracts used to finance equipment leases:

➲ **Conditional sales contract.** Under this arrangement, the purchaser does not take ownership of the equipment until it has been fully paid for.

➲ **Chattel-mortgage contract.** Here, the equipment becomes the property of the purchaser on delivery, but the seller holds a claim against it until the amount of the purchase contract has been paid in full.

Commercial leasing companies are listed in the yellow pages of your business-to-business telephone directory.

116. Return on investment

PROBLEM: You need more capital and are trying to interest some investors in your company, but you aren't sure how to prove to them it's a good opportunity.

DIAGNOSIS: Be prepared to show your potential investors that the company is providing a good return on investment.

PRESCRIPTION: To determine your company's return on investment, divide your net profit by the capital that you have invested in the company. The larger the return on investment, the more attractive the company will be to investors.

117. If you get a letter from the IRS...

PROBLEM: You receive a letter from the IRS questioning your tax return.

DIAGNOSIS: This is not a request. It's a command performance. Give it your prompt attention!

PRESCRIPTION: The least annoying letter is one that simply says that the IRS believes you've made a mistake on your tax return and asks for more money.

- Ask your tax preparer to go over your return to see if he or she agrees with the IRS's opinion.
- If you decide that the IRS is right, make the payment.
- If you believe the IRS is wrong and you don't owe any more money, send a letter explaining why you disagree.

Always send correspondence to the IRS by certified mail, return receipt requested. That will help you to prove, if necessary, that you responded in a timely manner.

Some situations are more difficult

If, on the other hand, the IRS thinks the situation requires a more thorough investigation, it will set up one of two types of audit:

- **An office visit**—where you visit an IRS office—is more convenient for you. It's usually less detailed.

- **A field visit** occurs when the IRS sends one of its field representatives to see you, probably because he or she wants to see more records than you could conveniently carry. In that case:
  - Provide only the information that you are asked for.
  - Answer only the questions that you are asked.
  - Don't raise issues the IRS hasn't raised. If you do, the audit may expand into areas that you aren't prepared to discuss.

Your accountant can represent you at an IRS audit meeting, as can almost anyone else who carries your power of attorney (use IRS Form 2848).

118. If you think the IRS is wrong...

PROBLEM: After going through an audit and reviewing all of the pertinent records in great detail, the IRS agent believes you owe the government more money, but you don't.

DIAGNOSIS: Then it's time to start the appeal process. There are three stages you can go through.

PRESCRIPTION: If you and the IRS auditor don't agree, ask for a meeting with your agent's supervisor. Failing to convince the auditor's supervisor that you are right, ask for a meeting with a representative of the Office of the Regional Director of Appeals.

If you go this far, you will have to file a formal protest, and you should be sure to involve your tax adviser and/or accountant at this point. Don't feel that you are fighting a losing battle, however; About 85 percent of the cases that go to the Regional Director are settled there. Settlement usually involves a compromise on the side of both parties, you and the government.

If you are one of the unfortunate 15 percent that still doesn't get any satisfaction—and you still maintain that you don't owe the government any additional money—the final step is to go to court. Unless it is a severe case, you might prefer to accept whatever settlement the Regional Director suggests, because court cases are costly and time-consuming—and you *still* can lose.

Another consideration: If you go to court and win, your attorney's fees may amount to more than the sum you would have had to pay the IRS. Why bother?

Chapter 12

When customers aren't happy

119. Why customers are lost

PROBLEM: Your company is losing customers and you're not sure why.

DIAGNOSIS: The American Society of Quality Control conducted a study to determine why a company loses customers. The answers are very revealing. According to the survey, the reasons are:

68%	Customer was turned away by the indifferent attitude of a company employee.
14%	Customer was dissatisfied with the product.
9%	Customer was lured away by competition.
5%	Customer was influenced by a friend to go elsewhere.
3%	Customer moves away.
1%	Death of the customer.

PRESCRIPTION: Because over two thirds of the problems (68 percent) are related to how employees deal with customers, you should:

- ➲ Concentrate your energy and effort on how employees are treating customers. Release those who are indifferent. Provide special rewards for those who are the most successful in keeping your customers satisfied.
- ➲ Use the word "customer" in as many job titles as possible.
- ➲ Measure customer reaction to how they are treated by your employees regularly.
- ➲ Personally observe how customer problems are resolved.
- ➲ Train, train, train.

120. Keys to customer satisfaction

PROBLEM: How do you keep your customers happy so they will bring you return business and recommend you to others?

DIAGNOSIS: Customer satisfaction, as nearly everybody knows, is the key to success in virtually every business. Finding new customers is a great deal more difficult than retaining the customers you have, so it is extremely important to please your customers in every way possible.

PRESCRIPTION: Here are a few suggestions that may not have occurred to you:

- ➲ **Turn down the job.** Sure, that's a pretty drastic approach, but it's better than taking the job and not being able to handle it as you should. If you try and fail, you'll disappoint—and probably lose—the customer. Sometimes, it's just not possible to satisfy a given customer at a given time. When that happens, you're better off to be upfront and admit it.
- ➲ **Analyze what your competition is doing.** See what your competitor is doing and do it better. Add some special service that your customer can't get anywhere else.
- ➲ **Stay in touch with your customers.** Use mailings, follow-up phone calls, personal thank-you notes or other devices to let the customer know you appreciate his business.
- ➲ **Ask your customers** if there's anything more you could have done to make them happy.
- ➲ **Offer special incentives** such as discounts, gift certificates or small promotional items to please the customer and ensure a favorable response whenever they need your services again.

121. Staying focused on your market

PROBLEM: After attaining a measure of success, your company has lost its focus and has been trying to be all things to all people.

DIAGNOSIS: It has been wisely said that you can't stand for anything if you chase after everything. If the company has temporarily lost its focus, try to get it back again.

Many entrepreneurs do not know how to grow their companies. They move away from their original business, rather than concentrating on the thing they do the best. They do not realize that they are more powerful when they have a narrow focus than if they have a bloated product line.

Often, after some initial success, a small company will attempt to increase sales by reorganizing itself into several small divisions and hiring new people to manage each one. Too often, after trying to change the company's focus, the company falters and dies.

PRESCRIPTION: A narrow focus is particularly valuable when a company is involved in one of the new industries. Consider IBM, which once had a virtual monopoly on computers, but when large mainframe systems gave way to inexpensive personal computers, small competitors with a narrower focus jumped into the field and took over the market.

➲ As a small company, unencumbered by rigid bureaucracy, procedures and precedents, you should be able to refocus your efforts with less trouble than a large company.

Refocusing requires:

• Objectivity.

• Courage.

• Sacrifice.

• The unanimous agreement of your key decision-makers.

➲ The time to refocus is when your sales begin to flatten or when you see new opportunities arise.

➲ Try refocusing on a second brand. If the company has two strong brands, it can have two strong focuses.

122. Customers buy perceived value

PROBLEM: You have lost 10 percent of your customers in the past year, even though your product has not changed and you have no new competitors.

DIAGNOSIS: An old marketing axiom says that you should "sell the sizzle, not the steak." In other words, offer the customer some "perceived value," not just a cold, lifeless piece of meat.

Automobiles are sold as "adventure on the open road," not as an assembly of nuts and bolts.

Clothing is sold for its ability to help the wearer seem more attractive, not as an artful arrangement of colored cloth.

PRESCRIPTION: A perception of good value comes from a variety of things, depending on the nature of the product. These include the way in which the product is packaged, the price of the product and even the appearance of the place where the product is sold (or of the individual selling it).

Some ways in which you can give your customers an enhanced feeling that your company offers good value include:

- Offering the customer something extra:
  - Free gift-wrapping is a common example.
- Satisfying a customer's need for comfort, convenience, status, security or adventure.
- Stressing quality:
  - A product that performs well and demonstrates long life offers a powerful sales incentive.
  - Consistency is important. Customers like to know that the quality will be the same every time they buy your product.
  - Honesty is also important. Customers appreciate being told the truth about what they will receive and when. Failing to fulfill a promise is one of the surest ways to lose a customer.
- Meeting or exceeding customers' expectations:
  - Be sure that the customer receives as much or more than expected.
  - Be sure that the customer gets *what* he or she has ordered *on time*.
  - Be sure that the customers gets *what* was ordered *the way he or she wants it*. If the customer has ordered rare, don't give him well-done.
  - Be sure your product compares favorably with your competitor's product.
  - Be sure your product compares favorably with what you have advertised. This reflects back on the question of honesty.
- Engaging salespeople or company representatives who are helpful to the customer:
  - Be sure your representatives demonstrate a good attitude and are responsive to your customers.
  - Customers like to deal with those who are knowledgeable, can answer their questions, demonstrate care and concern, and are pleasant to deal with.

The more measurable these benefits are, the more value the customer feels that he or she is getting when he or she patronizes your business.

123. Know the competition

PROBLEM: Your sales are falling; your competitor's sales are rising.

DIAGNOSIS: It's time to analyze your competition and try to determine what they are offering that you're not. Then you can take whatever action is necessary.

PRESCRIPTION: Here is a minimal checklist for you to follow as you compare your company against your competitor(s):

➲ **Is your competitor better known?**
  - Is the company older?
  - Is the company larger?
  - Does it do more advertising than you do?
  - Is its promotional activity, including advertising, better than yours?
  - If you can't outspend your competitor in advertising, concentrate on quality, customer satisfaction and service. These are the best advertising you can produce.

➲ **Is there something your competitor has overlooked?**
  - If your competitor has a weakness, exploit it.

➲ **What is your competitor doing that's *not* working?**
  - Listen for complaints from your competitor's customers. Be sure your company isn't guilty of making the same mistakes.
  - Make a list of the competitor's weak points. Can these things be used to your advantage?

➲ **How good is your service?**
  - Is your competitor making it easier for customers to do business with them? How?
  - Follow up faithfully on any customer complaints or criticisms. Repeat business is critical.
  - Use outside agencies to objectively evaluate your customer service and employees.

⮑ **How does your competitor set prices?**
- Are your prices higher?
- Does your competitor offer customers more for the dollar than you do?
- If you can't compete favorably in everything your competitor does, pick out the areas in which you *can* offer superior price, quality or service.

There are a number of ways to acquire this kind of competitor intelligence:

⮑ Performing on-site inspections.
⮑ Buying your competitor's products:
- Test them.
- Take them apart.
- Have your own employees analyze them for quality and cost.

⮑ Talking to the competitor's employees.
⮑ Talking to the competitor's customers.
⮑ Talking to the competitor's suppliers.
⮑ Talking to the competitor's banker.
⮑ Talking to a securities analyst.
⮑ Reading the competitor's advertising.
⮑ Geting a copy of the annual report, if the competitor is a publicly owned company,
⮑ Purchasing a share of the competitor's stock, which puts you on several mailing lists to receive the latest shareholder information.
⮑ Hiring a clipping service to send you material from the media. The cost will run about $110 per month for one competitor plus 55 cents per clipping; adding another competitor should increase the cost about $10 a month.
⮑ Seeing what you can learn through one of the computerized information services:
- Dow Jones News Retrieval Service.
- New York Times Information Bank.
- Industry news.
- Financial news.
- Historical data.

➲ Hiring a professional market research firm, which can provide you with such information as:

- What the competitor is doing in the way of research and development.
- New patent filings that have been made.
- New product announcements.
- Product sales data.
- The competitor's profit and loss statements.

A competitor's labor contract expiration dates and plant closes can indicate that it will experience a slowdown or cessation in production, which will create a greater demand for your products.

Learning about pending legal entanglements, antitrust actions and changes in your competitor's top personnel can also tell you things that might have an impact on your business.

At the same time, take steps to be sure that your own secrets are held fail-safe:

- In appropriate situations, require employees to sign patent, secrecy or noncompetition agreements.
- Caution employees not to discuss important company business outside the office.
- Protect your premises from outsiders.
- Conduct interviews with employees who have had access to company secrets before they leave the company and remind them of their signed agreements.

124. How to get the facts you need

PROBLEM: With declining sales, you know you're not satisfying customer needs, but you honestly aren't sure what they want. Is it quality, price, competition, reliability, packaging, service?

DIAGNOSIS: If you feel you're lacking information, go out and get some. If you can't afford to engage a professional organization to conduct the survey, you can conduct your own.

PRESCRIPTION: Follow these pointers and you can conduct a very revealing customer survey on your own:

➲ Be honest about your intentions. Tell your respondents why you are conducting the survey and what you intend to do with the information that you gather.

- Be polite.

- Ask the same set of questions of every participant.

- Be sure your questions are brief, clear and unambiguous.

- Keep the overall questionnaire as short as possible. If you can't get all of the information you want with one survey, conduct another survey to acquire the rest.

- Ask questions that can be answered with a yes or a no, if possible.

- Do not phrase questions to address more than one issue at a time.

- Do everything possible to avoid bias in your questions.

- If you address more than one issue in the questionnaire, batch the questionnaires so that all questions related to each issue will be asked consecutively.

- Make the questionnaire attractive and easy to read. Double or triple space. Leave wide margins. Use readable type. Avoid colored inks. Keep it simple.

- Give respondents time to answer your questions. Be sure their answers are understandable.

Chapter 13

Change before you have to

125. Picking a niche in the market

PROBLEM: You have an idea for a new product, but you aren't sure how it would be received in the market. Time and money to find out are limited.

DIAGNOSIS: For every product, there is a unique niche for it in the market. The trick is to find that niche.

PRESCRIPTION: To take a new product or innovation to market successfully, see if it fits one of these descriptions:

- **Being the first with the most.** Example: The first company to sell bite-size candy bars by the sackful. Prior to that, candy bars were candy bars and sack candy was sack candy.

- **Hitting the competition "where it ain't."** Example: Putting wheels on luggage for easier handling. Previously, you had to buy a fold-up cart to put your luggage on.

- **Finding an ecological niche.** Companies are manufacturing shopping bags from recycled paper, reducing the need to harvest more trees.

- **Changing the economic characteristics of the product.** Example: The entire range of disposables—razor blades, Kleenex, milk cartons, plastic eating utensils, containers for hot and cold drinks, napkins, shower caps, tablecloths, hypodermic needles and other medical supplies, slippers and other hospital supplies, spray-paint containers, and so on.

➲ **Changing the economic characteristics of the market.** Example: First, the Volkswagen, and more recently, the Geo Metro. In years past, auto-mobiles were big and substantial; now (partly due to ecological concerns) the emphasis is on small, inexpensive cars that produce more miles to a gallon of gas.

126. Testing customer reaction

PROBLEM: You have a new product you're very enthusiastic about. But before you spend lots of money to launch it, how will you know the market will be equally enthusiastic?

DIAGNOSIS: A little test-marketing can be very helpful. What you do with the information you get from test-marketing can be crucial.

PRESCRIPTION: The purpose of test-marketing is simple: to produce *and attempt to sell* some of your new product to see if *real people* will actually spend *real money* to buy it. This means asking potential purchasers of the product:

➲ Do you like my product?

➲ If so, what would you be willing to pay for it *if it were available in a local store*?

➲ If it were available in a local store *at the price you have said you would be willing to pay for it*, would you:

  (a) Definitely buy it?

  (b) Possibly buy it?

  (c) Not buy it?

➲ How many times a year would you buy it?

➲ Are you using a similar product now?

➲ Are you happy with your present product?

➲ If so, why would you switch to my product?

In the process of gathering this information, also gather demographic information about your respondents, including:

➲ Age.

➲ Sex.

➲ Race/nationality.

➲ Marital status.

➲ Education.

➲ Occupation.

➲ Income level.

All of this can be helpful to you when you are developing your marketing strategy later on. *Once you have gathered the information, digest it and evaluate the data.*

Could you produce the product profitably?

During your interviews, you asked people what they would pay for your product. Throw out the top 10 percent and the bottom 10 percent of the prices that were mentioned to you. Answers in the mid-range will be more realistic.

Take those mid-range answers and average them. The result will tell you the potential customer's "perceived value" of your product and that should be your sales price, at least at the outset.

Next, deduct the amount that the retail store probably will want for its markup on the product:

> Something you eat, drink
>   or use to clean with................25%
> An appliance, household
>   item or cosmetic item............35%
> Something sold in a
>   hardware or specialty store...40%

For a more accurate answer, ask three or four local merchants what markup they would place on your type of product.

Now subtract 15 percent for what it will cost you to sell the product to the store (sales salaries or commissions, etc.); 10 percent more for warehousing and transportation; 15 percent for advertising the product; and 10 percent to cover administrative and miscellaneous costs. Whatever is left is what you can spend to manufacture the product and (hopefully) salt away for profit.

Is there a legitimate market for the product?

Gather the data from your "Would you buy?" question.

Count *all* of those who said that they would *definitely* buy your product and *half* of those who said that they *would possibly* buy your product. Compare that figure to the total number of people interviewed. If the result is:

> 85% or higher....You have a winner!
> 65% to 85%........Your chances are good.
> 50% to 65%........There's a possibility.
> Under 50%.........Forget it!

Now comes the real test

To go beyond the "what if" stage, you will need to have some samples of the actual product. You can make them yourself or, if that's not possible, have somebody make some for you.

Decide how to package the product. An advertising agency can help you design an appealing package, or you can talk to a packaging company that has a design department that can help you.

If your product will be sold to industrial users, ask a sales agent who has an established clientele in that industry to test the product with some of his or her customers.

More likely, your product will be sold through retail outlets. If so:

➲ Make and package enough of the product to stock a half-dozen outlets.

➲ Ask some independently owned retailers in your comunity if they will allow you to put up a display in their store for a little while. If you don't charge them anything for your product, that will be an incentive for them to cooperate.

➲ Be sure to set up your exhibit in the area where products similar to yours are being exhibited. Your objective is to see how your product compares with the others.

➲ At the end of the specified test period, ask the retailer not only to tell you how many of your product were sold, but to tell you how many of *each competitor's* products were sold during the test period. This will give you some idea of how much market share your product may be able to attain.

   If your product outsold the top competitor, obviously you have a winner. If it undersold its weakest competitor, you should reconsider taking the product to market.

➲ If the product has sold reasonably well, ask each of the cooperating retailers to consider keeping the item on display in the store. If more than half of them agree, you have reason to be excited.

If all of the signs have been good thus far, you're now ready to put the product on the market.

127. How to market a new product

PROBLEM: You are trying to decide how to advertise a new product and discover you still haven't determined its market niche.

DIAGNOSIS: It is dangerous to spend money advertising before either surveying potential buyers or testing whether people will actually buy it and at what price. You can do this with little expense and low risk—in one community, a few outlets and small sampling.

PRESCRIPTION: Test-marketing is more revealing than a survey because it actually requires the respondent to spend money on your product, whereas a survey only asks if *the respondent would be likely to buy the product* if it were available.

If you cannot afford to engage a professional test-marketing organization, you can conduct your own study:

- ➲ Set up a small booth and position it in a high-traffic area.
- ➲ Ask a store in your community to carry the item for a short period of time. To increase the chances of acceptance, allow them to take the product on consignment.

However you manage to sell the product, be sure to follow up with the purchasers. Try to determine:

- ➲ How they liked the product.
- ➲ Whether there were any features about the product that they did *not* like.
- ➲ Whether the product was reasonably priced.
- ➲ Whether they would recommend the product to friends.
- ➲ How you might improve the product.

Analytically—and objectively—study the opinions that the customers give you. Act on any that would seem to make the product more marketable.

128. How to launch a new product

PROBLEM: You have developed and test-marketed a new product and still think you have a winner. How can you be sure?

DIAGNOSIS: The first step is behind you. From this point on, the job calls for dedication, hard work and persistence. If the product has any potential, you will find out soon enough.

PRESCRIPTION: At this point, it is important for you to know the parameters of your potential market.

How many products similar to yours are sold each year? Contact a trade association that covers such products and ask to see its data on sales. If it won't share the information with you freely, then you can ask your advertising agency to get the information for you or you may have to invest in the cost of a membership.

A trade association can tell you what major sales outlets are for your type of product, and what share of the market each outlet enjoys.

Now perform some mathematics: If, as in the test-marketing example cited previously, you have learned that a half-dozen outlets sold 100 units of all types during a two-week test period, and that six of them were yours, you could suppose that you are capable of capturing 10 percent of the market on a national basis.

If you now take the national sales figure given to you by the trade association, multiply it by your 10-percent market share and multiply that by the unit sales price of your product, you can estimate your dollar sales volume *nationally* over a comparable sales period.

Caution: It may be tempting to "annualize" your sales total simply by taking your two-week test-market figure and multiplying it by 26. However, many products do not sell equally well from month-to-month; for example, sweaters sell much better in the winter than they do in the summer, and they sell much better in the north than they do in the south. Take such factors into account when you try to arrive at a realistic forecast of your potential *annual* sales volume.

Using this information, you can begin to think about such things as a pattern of distribution for your product. If you forecast annual sales of $20 million or more, the supermarkets might be interested in handling your product; if not, look for other outlets. If the forecast is for $4 million to $20 million, perhaps department stores or mass retailers like Kmart will take an interest in handling your product.

Engage someone to help you create a marketing plan. Through it, you will learn:

- ➲ How much it will cost—to do what and when.
- ➲ How quickly—or slowly—you should bring out your product.
- ➲ Whether you should introduce the product market by market, rather than taking it national at the start.
- ➲ How much to spend on advertising and promotion.
- ➲ How much product you will need—and when.

From this, you can develop your overall business plan, including sales forecasts, financial requirements, and so on.

129. Pricing your product or service

PROBLEM: You are ready to go to market with your new product or service, but you're not sure how to price it.

DIAGNOSIS: Failing to cover all of your operating expenses will result in underpricing, a loss of profit and possible financial ruin.

Look into your competitor's pricing policies. Should you use the same policies or another policy? Why?

Most important, will your pricing strategy enable your product to be competitive in the marketplace?

Are you planning to offer customers a large-volume discount? If so, have you established a rational policy for it?

Is your pricing policy likely to change in the future? Why? When? How?

PRESCRIPTION: The two most common pricing techniques are:

○ **Skimming.** This technique "skims the top of the market" and is useful to the company that is introducing a unique product or service. Since it has virtually no competition, this product can carry a high price and can be aimed at a select audience. As a prestige item, the product is favored by those who can afford to pay a high price to purchase a new or unusual item. Your profits are high, providing you with capital for growth, expansion and new product development.

Caution: Because of the high profits the product generates, it will attract imitators. Some of them will compete by selling their product at a lower price, which will drive prices down. If you select this pricing strategy, you must be prepared to change price quickly in order to meet this new competition.

○ **Cost-plus.** This pricing strategy requires you to calculate the cost of your product, then add a set percentage of that figure on top of the cost to establish an acceptable level of profit. This is the strategy most commonly used by retailers.

Example: Begin by dividing your overhead by your total sales volume to determine your overhead on a per-unit basis. To that figure, you must then add the per-unit cost of the product.

Overhead = $60,000
divided by
Total Sales Volume = 10,000 units
equals
Overhead Per Unit = $6
plus
Cost of Product = $10 per unit
equals
Total Cost Per Unit = $16

Now add a preestablished amount of gross profit, say 25 percent.

Cost = $16 per unit
times
Gross Profit = 25 percent
equals
Gross Profit = $4 per unit

By adding the cost per unit ($16) and the gross profit per unit ($4), you arrive at a sales price of $20 per unit.

Sometimes, the profit margin is expressed as a percentage of the total cost in these calculations, rather than as a markup on purchases.

130. Preparing a customer proposal

PROBLEM: A potentially important customer has asked you to submit a proposal—something you have never done in your life. Without one, however, there isn't a prayer of getting the customer's business.

DIAGNOSIS: Assuming the customer did not give you a specific format to follow, we will outline one here. Before you start work on the proposal, however, be absolutely sure you have every detail of the proposed deal at your fingertips.

PRESCRIPTION: To prepare a businesslike proposal, follow these pointers:

What the proposal should include

- State the purpose of your proposal in the first sentence.
- Define the situation as it now stands. Be sure it reflects the customer's *need* to conclude this sale, but stick to the facts. Don't embroider or speculate.
- List all of the customer's objectives and describe how you propose to help meet them. Use the customer's own words, when possible, to show that you were listening and paying attention.
- If it's relevant, give your background. Show how you have been able to help others, not how wonderful you are.
- Describe how the sales process will occur. Specify exactly who will do what and when. Mention the dates on which these commitments were made.

- Include a list of all the products or services you offer, itemized in a logical order.
- State the cost and the value attached to the cost, that is, the return on investment or the productivity payback involved.
- Specify the terms, and be sure they are stated exactly as you discussed them with the customer before the proposal was written. Allow no opportunity for misinterpretation or misunderstanding.

Give the proposal an attractive appearance

- On the supposition that your customer will be receiving other proposals, try to make yours stand out.
- The cover should be something that will make people want to turn it over and look inside.
- Put the customer's logo on the cover, too.
- Use short paragraphs for clarity and emphasis.
- Boldface important material.
- Edit the material carefully to be sure it is accurate, complete and free of typing errors. Delete unnecessary words, including about half of the adjectives and adverbs.
- Use bullets and similar attention-getting devices.
- Use paper that's heavy enough that the type on the following page doesn't show through.
- Use a good, readable typeface.
- Put a big "thank you" at the end of the proposal.
- Add an approval page for your customer to sign—and be sure your signature is already on it.
- Attach testimonial letters and references in the event someone who has not heard your presentation would like to do some additional checking.
- Include something unexpected, like an article that pertains to your customer or his or her business.
- Don't just staple your proposal together; enclose it in a high-quality binding.

And finally...

- Ask someone informed but impartial to go over your proposal and offer suggestions for improvements.
- Ask for a response by a specific date.
- Sign the letter with your first name only.

⊃ Prepare a sparkling cover letter—short, sweet and readable. Do not "resell" your proposal here, just strive to be professional, competent and willing to serve.

⊃ See that the proposal is delivered in a meaningful manner:
- Personal hand-delivery is best.
- Someone from your company would be next best.
- A courier service will suffice.
- If nothing else, use Overnight or Priority Mail.

131. Coping with a shifting market

PROBLEM: Sales are plummeting and the market reflects a negative feeling about your product. To clear out excess stock, your salespeople are clamoring for you to do more advertising and make more pricing concessions. The production people are preparing for a wave of cutbacks and layoffs. The people in finance want to limit losses and protect the balance sheet by slashing budgets.

DIAGNOSIS: You are having troubles—but buck up. If you tackle the situation head-on, you probably can fight your way back in less time than you think. But don't delay, because every day you wait to fight back, the harder the task will be.

PRESCRIPTION: Nobody can get to the root of your problems more accurately or quickly than your customers.

⊃ **Engage a professional research firm to interview your customers.** A professional research firm knows how to extract the information that you need in the shortest time possible. It can help you to frame the right questions and design the necessary market samples.

⊃ **Use focus groups.** In such a group, a facilitator can quiz your customers to uncover attitudes that might remain hidden under more structured types of questioning.

⊃ **Send your executives and your salespeople out to talk to the customers.** Compare their findings with those from the professionals, the focus groups and other kinds of surveys.

⊃ **Go out into the field yourself.** Many customers will speak more openly to the CEO than they will to a subordinate or to a professional research team.

➲ **Establish what your problem is.** From the information that you are gathering, begin to formulate your conclusions. Keep refining your approach until all of the data is in and/or you have run out of time. Your main purpose is to determine whether you are selling a product that:

- Has a design flaw.

- Does not measure up to specifications.

- Is well-engineered, but is failing for want of a better marketing program.

- Is well-engineered and well-marketed, but is not in tune with current tastes, desires and needs.

- Suffers from some combination of the above.

➲ **Prepare to take corrective action.** If the product is no longer viable, kill it. Cut your losses.

If the product does have a future, you need to decide how much you are willing to spend on reestablishing it and how much time you have to do it.

Adjust your production levels until you have the problem corrected; there's no sense increasing your inventory. Decrease your inventory and generate more cash by trying to balance production against sales.

Revise your financial forecasts conservatively; your situation will only worsen if you suffer a cash crisis before you have your product problem solved. Let your lenders and creditors know about your revisions—and your intentions.

➲ **Fix your problem.** If your product design is subpar, redesign it.

- After your product design people have developed a new design, ask your salespeople if they think it will fly.

- See if finance thinks you can afford to reintroduce the product.

- If everyone is in agreement, launch the product again.

If inadequate marketing has been your problem, look for a new approach.

- Your advertising agency can handle a simple change of message.

- New packaging may help.

- See if you can identify a new market niche for the product.

If your distribution system is weak or unable to finance and service your product, you have a problem that may take years to correct.

- The only speedy solution may be to buy out or merge with someone who can provide the capability you need.

➲ **Return to the market**. When the timing seems right, return to the marketplace with your redesigned product and your enhanced marketing program.

- Invade your competitors' territory at its weak points.

- Win back your customers.

- Be committed, and put up the resources needed to do the job properly. Coming back may prove to be harder than it was to get in.

- Increase production slowly, trying to stay just a bit behind. Protect your pricing.

➲ **A shifting market.** If the market has lost interest in your product, there's not a great deal that can be done, even when you have a good product.

- See if you can reposition your product by identifying and pursuing a totally new market. (Silly Putty was originally developed as a rubber substitute during World War II. When it failed in that, an enterprising employee bought the patent and put it on the market *as a children's plaything*.)

- If another market niche cannot be found, stop production, sell your remaining inventory for whatever you can get and turn your attention to other pursuits. If you have been a leader in the market, you do not necessarily have to lose your position in it simply because one product has run its course.

132. Will it sell to the government?

PROBLEM: With the billions upon billions of dollars that the government spends at the local, county, state and federal levels, there must be some way to get a piece of the action.

DIAGNOSIS: Right! And now there are new regulations to help cut through the red tape, new policies and "a new attitude" (Washington's terms, not ours) that are said to make it easier than ever to sell your wares to such agencies as the Department of Defense (DOD), particularly if you are a company operated by a woman or a member of a minority.

PRESCRIPTION: For a broader view of the opportunities that may be available for making sales to the government, see my book *Nobody Gets Rich Working for Somebody Else*, mentioned previously.

For brevity, let's examine the "new" situation at the Department of Defense:

- ➲ **Get a CAGE number.** To do business with any base or other entity under the DOD, you will need a Commercial and Government Entity (CAGE) number. This is now the basic vendor number for you to use.

   To get a CAGE number, you must fill out DD Form 2051. It is a simple one-page form that can be obtained, along with instructions on how to fill it out, by calling your nearest base and asking for the Small Business Purchasing Officer. If it is more convenient, you can get the form by visiting the nearest office of the Small Business Administration.

   You no longer will have to have a separate vendor number for each base with which you wish to do business.

- ➲ List yourself with the appropriate Small Business purchasing officer *at each location* with which you plan to do business. When you are talking to the Small Business purchasing officer about obtaining the form to apply for a CAGE number, ask to be sent a Standard Form 129, Solicitation Mailing List Application. Be sure to say that you are a potential contractor or supplier.

   This form tells the purchasing officer at the specific facility with which you plan to do business that you want to be on their bid list to sell your products/services. You must submit a separate SF 129 to each facility with which you want to do business.

- ➲ **Subscribe to the new Electronic Data Interchange.** The DOD is moving toward a "paperless office" approach for just about all purchases through an Electronic Data Interchange. The objective is to handle all of the department's purchasing needs electronically *around the world*, from offer to bid to contract.

   This Interchange will be accessed through a new, online network to which you can now subscribe. Until the system is fully operational, however, you may be asked to sign up with another service on a temporary basis.

The local base purchasing officer will help you to get on one of these networks, and you should do so as quickly as possible. When the system is fully operational, you will need a computer with a modem, telephone connections and the related hardware if you wish to participate in bidding for DOD contracts.

133. Can you take it overseas?

PROBLEM: You have a product that should sell as well overseas as it does in the United States, but you're not familiar with international marketing.

DIAGNOSIS: With the passage of NAFTA, the dissolution of the Iron Curtain bloc, the Common Market movement in Europe and a rapidly growing economy around the Pacific Rim, there can be no doubt that the international arena is "where it's at" today. If you're not investigating the potential already, you had better start to do so.

PRESCRIPTION: There is a ton of support for those who are prepared to make the commitment to international marketing. Among others, these resources include:

- Local, state and national chambers of commerce.
- College and university international business centers.
- Various Economic Development Councils at the local, regional and state levels.
- State Departments of Commerce.
- Various Export-Import and Foreign Trade Councils, usually operated at the state level.
- Various state World Trade Associations.
- U.S. Small Business Administration.
- International Trade Administration, U.S. Department of Commerce.
- U.S. Department of Commerce, U.S. & Foreign Commerce Service (US&FCS).
- U.S. Customs Service.
- The trade specialists in American embassies throughout the world.
- Trade specialists who are working in the embassies of various foreign countries in cities throughout the United States.

- ➲ American Association of Exporters and Importers, Chicago.
- ➲ National Association of Export Companies, New York City.
- ➲ National Customs Brokers & Forwarders Association of America, New York City.
- ➲ U.S. Council of the International Chamber of Commerce, New York City.
- ➲ World Trade Institute, New York City.
- ➲ The American Management Association has an International Division headquartered in New York City.
- ➲ Many states maintain foreign trade offices in various countries throughout the world as a service to businesses that are located within their boundaries.
- ➲ Many large banks have an international department that can provide a great deal of information and assistance.
- ➲ Large international shippers, such as Federal Express, also can be helpful.
- ➲ A number of helpful books, including my own *How to Export* (Probus Publishing Co.), are available at your local public library or bookstore.

Various government publications also are available for the asking, including:

How to Expand Your Market Through Exporting (Pub. #2004)

U.S. Chamber of Commerce
Publications Fulfillment
1610 H St., NW
Washington, DC 20062

Market Overseas with U.S. Government Help
(Management Aids #7.003)

U.S. Small Business Administration
Office of International Trade
1441 L St., NW, Suite 501A
Washington, DC 20416

The World Is Your Market

U.S. Small Business Administration
Office of International Trade
1441 L St., NW, Suite 501A
Washington, DC 20416

International Trade Assistance (SBA Fact Sheet #42)

U.S. Small Business Administration
Office of International Trade
1441 L St., NW, Suite 501A
Washington, DC 20416

Facts About AID

Agency for International Development
Washington, DC 20523-1414

Export Opportunities with the Agency for International Development

Agency for International Development
Washington, DC 20523-1414

AID Importer List

Agency for International Development
Washington, DC 20523-1414

How to Get the Most From Overseas Exhibitions

U.S. Department of Commerce, US&FCS
Room H 2116
Washington, DC 20230

134. Getting beyond survival

PROBLEM: With good cash flow, a solid customer base and an optimistic profit picture, you are anxious to grow and spread out. Dreams of becoming tomorrow's Wal-Mart or Blockbuster Video are dancing in your head. But how to take the next step?

DIAGNOSIS: Congratulations on coming this far! Now is the time to consolidate your current position and contemplate future possibilities slowly and carefully. Don't do anything impulsive!

If you have attained at least a 20-percent market share, it may be time to spread out. But if your share of the market is down in the 5-percent to 10-percent range, you probably would be well-advised not to take on anything more. Concentrate on what you do best.

Success in one venture does not mean that you're invincible! Business is like a crapshoot: You can have a winner on the first roll and snake-eyes on the next.

PRESCRIPTION: Don't make unilateral decisions. Consult your advisers. Listen to a variety of views and gather as much information as possible before you decide on a course of action.

In general terms, there are four ways you can go:

➲ **Business as usual.** That is, keep doing essentially what you have been, increasing the business gradually by constantly adding to the number of customers that you serve. This may not be the most dramatic decision, but it's certainly one of the safest. Strive to dominate your market over the long haul.

➲ **Instead of adding more customers, strengthen your relationship with the customers you already have**. Stress quality, customer service and new products. Make your company indispensable to its customers and get those customers to purchase more and more merchandise from you as the years go on. This is an excellent tactic if your customers are in a growth mode. You grow right along with them. But if they are declining, eventually they will take you right along with them.

➲ **Restructure your business to allow for easy expansion** during good times and easy contraction during slowdowns. There are a number of ways to do this. One is to outsource almost everything, rather than handle everything in-house. That will make your company lean and mean—consisting of a small core of key employees, rather than a work force that is constantly expanding.

➲ **Take on more "partners."** Spin off parts of the company, forming subsidiaries. Set up some joint ventures with other companies (both customers and suppliers are likely business partners). Create other partnerships. These tactics help you to spread out the risk of further expansion. They also lessen the headaches of management— specifically, trying to take on too much at one time.

135. What growth demands

PROBLEM: As the business grows, there are more and more details to contend with. It's easy and tempting to lose track of important details.

DIAGNOSIS: There are three ways to contend with a burgeoning mass of business details: computerization, frequent analysis and asking your key people to give you a hand.

PRESCRIPTION: You can't expect your employees to be disciplined and to keep a watch over details unless you set a good example. These areas are vital:

➲ **Computerize.** Computers can give you a handy, fast, accurate means of updating your inventory, managing your accounting, and keeping a vast array of other important data. Perhaps over-the-counter software will be sufficient; if not, an accounting firm can modify it to meet your needs.

➲ **Analyze your results.** You should analyze your inventory once or twice a month. Do it weekly during periods of strong sales growth or waning orders.

Analyze various financial reports according to a carefully established schedule that has been designed to help you find potential trouble spots *before* they get out of hand.

➲ **Key people can help you.** But you have to see that they have prompt access to accurate information and they know that their suggestions for improvement will be welcomed and acted upon promptly.

136. Family ties and binds

PROBLEM: After operating a small business with the assistance of your family for several years, you are beginning to consider expansion. But you're also beginning to realize that expansion may be more difficult in a family business.

DIAGNOSIS: Expanding a business is often contrasted with simply operating a business, in the same way that planning ahead is contrasted with day-to-day living. It requires a great deal more long-range thinking—and paying attention to a broader range of considerations.

PRESCRIPTION: My book, *The Entrepreneurial Family* (McGraw-Hill, Inc.), discusses all aspects of starting, operating and ultimately stepping down from a family-owned business.

Of particular interest to those who may be planning to expand such a business is this list of questions:

➲ For and about spouses:
  • What if your spouse gets disabled and can't work?
  • What if your spouse decides to leave the company and go into another line of work?

- What if there is a divorce?
- What if your health—or your spouse's health—turns bad?
- Do you and your spouse agree on when and how you will retire?
- Do you and your spouse agree on how to dispose of the business when you (a) retire, or (b) pass away?

➲ For and about parents:
- What should you do when your children go to college? Get married? Go into some other line of work?
- Are you sure the children *want* to take over the family business?
- Are you sure the children are *capable* of taking over the family business?
- Without the income from the business, will you be able to retire comfortably?

➲ For and about the children:
- What if Mom and Dad retire, leaving you alone to run the business?
- What if Mom and Dad were to die suddenly?
- What if Mom and Dad were to sell the business?
- Do you really *want* to make a career of this business?
- Is there sufficient growth potential in the business to sustain the living needs of an additional generation?

Attempt to answer these questions honestly and objectively. Then make your plans accordingly, taking all of the facts into consideration. These questions might help you to focus your thinking:

➲ Are you planning to expand the business for your own benefit, or are you doing it to accommodate your children, who may not be interested in continuing the business once you have stepped aside?

➲ Would the time, money and energy that you plan to put into expanding the business serve you better if it were expended elsewhere?

➲ How far away is retirement? If it's close at hand, will investing in an expansion of the business short-change your retirement program?

137. Growing too fast

PROBLEM: Your company grew at such a fast pace that your plant, equipment and manpower weren't able to cope with it. Is it possible to grow too fast?

DIAGNOSIS: Indeed it is, and inexperienced management can have a terrible time coping with it. Mismanaged success has destroyed more than one promising young company.

PRESCRIPTION: Be particularly careful when you arrange for additional financing. Agreeing to high interest rates because you believe yourself to be in a time-bind can result in terrible burdens upon the business later on.

Think long-term. Will this growth continue or is this merely a flash in the pan? How long can you expect this growth to continue— and at what rate?

➲ What is your *real* need for additional plant, equipment and manpower at this time? Expand as necessary, but don't begin building monuments. This is no time to go on an ego trip.

➲ Maybe you should consider subcontracting some of your work, or leasing some new facilities rather than buying or building them.

➲ If you expand now, how long will it be before you will need to expand again?

➲ Once your growth rate begins to level off, will you still need all of the plant, equipment and personnel that you're now considering?

Now, more than ever, is the time to be cautious and seek qualified outside assistance. Whatever the cost, it probably will be worth it, and if your business is really doing all that well, you should be able to afford it.

An additional caution: When a new product becomes extremely popular, it usually tends to attract competition. Sometimes the competitors will overpopulate the market and sometimes they will engage in price-cutting, which erodes the product's profitability.

Chapter 14

Avoiding trouble

138. Keeping partners together

PROBLEM: A group of individuals, all college classmates, former co-workers and good friends formed a company and went into business for themselves. Three years later, the partners stopped talking to each other, stopped working together and dissolved their business.

DIAGNOSIS: This sad story is too frequently repeated. An intense kind of closeness develops when a business partnership is formed, and when the inevitable business problems arise, they can easily lead to bitterness, misunderstandings, hurt feelings, anger, bruised egos and recriminations.

PRESCRIPTION: To avoid such disaster, details should be worked out—and agreed upon—by the partners *in advance,* at the time their original agreement is signed.

First, they should agree that everything will be shared equally:

- The workload.
- The expenses.
- The risks.
- The rewards.

Next, agreement should be reached on:

- How should the money be managed?
- What happens if it becomes necessary to skip a payday?
- What happens if extra capital is needed?
- Who is to handle what duties on a regular basis?
- Is the workload equally distributed?
- If somebody needs help, where should he or she turn?
- What if someone wants a day off?

The partners must commit to holding weekly management meetings.

- ➲ Consider each partner's attendance mandatory. If someone *must* miss a meeting, take no action involving his or her area of responsibility (passing along a suggestion or recommendation is allowed).
- ➲ Be honest with each other. Avoid the temptation to inflate either your successes or your failures.
- ➲ Never dismiss, ignore or avoid bad news.
- ➲ Face the tough issues together. Don't put a heavy burden on one individual alone; let everyone offer their ideas.
- ➲ Share the successes—and the failures.
- ➲ Be lavish in passing out praise; miserly in assigning blame.
- ➲ Take meeting minutes.
  - Be as specific and as detailed as possible.
  - See that everybody gets a personal copy.
  - See that everyone follows the agreements that were set forth—no exceptions, regardless of how minor.

Partners must be as conscientious about making their *partnership* work as they are about making their *business* work.

139. Good partners are hard to find

PROBLEM: After a number of years of working with your partner, she unexpectedly dies, leaving you on your own. The business is too much for you to handle alone and besides, you enjoyed the numerous benefits of sharing the business with a partner. Now you would like to find someone else who would be willing to enter the business with you.

DIAGNOSIS: No two people are alike, and the odds of finding someone else exactly like your previous partner are pretty slim. Expect the new partner to have his or her own way of doing things, values, and concepts, not only of where your business should be going but how to get there.

PRESCRIPTION: Seek a partner whose skills and interests supplement and complement your own. Someone too much like yourself will not be nearly as helpful as someone who can contribute additional skills and ideas to the firm.

- ⊃ In what areas do you need the most help?
- ⊃ What experience has the potential partner had in those areas?
- ⊃ What has been his or her success rate in those areas?
- ⊃ Has he or she demonstrated the ability to solve problems in ways that are acceptable to you and your clientele?
- ⊃ What kind of personality does the potential partner have? Will it blend well with your own?

Check the potential partner's resume and references in detail. If anything raises a red flag, ask about it, discuss it, then check to see if the explanation he or she gave you is accurate.

Finally, don't sell anyone a piece of your business too cheaply. Remember that you already have invested a great deal of time and effort in it, developed a client base, established a reputation, and invested money in such things as furniture, equipment and inventory.

Consider the possibility of allowing the individual to phase into partnership according to a preestablished and mutually agreeable set of conditions that must be met before this new position is fully vested.

140. Your worry is contagious

PROBLEM: Unsettled business conditions have you worried and you are concerned that your preoccupation with those worries may affect your work and that of your associates.

DIAGNOSIS: Businesses run most smoothly when they can be kept on a steady course, but unexpected problems do occur occasionally, and they naturally tend to divert the owner's attention from routine operations.

If at all possible, you should not let your concerns spread throughout the organization.

PRESCRIPTION: Approach business problems rationally and logically, not emotionally. If you become too emotional, fear can diminish your ability to recall the things that you actually know— things that can help you resolve your problems. People tend to run away from situations that contain too many fear-producing elements. On occasion, they may strike out in retaliation and become belligerent toward others, attempting to get even. Some, on the other hand, may tend to become unusually defensive.

When fear reaches your subordinates, they may react in the same way. Timid people tend to cling to rumors and exchange "sick" humor. Others tend to become bootlickers and informers, or to find other ways in which to flatter the superiors they perceive to be the source of their fear. Among the fearful, cliques and cabals tend to form.

Virtually all of these responses are counterproductive and should be discouraged. If you allow your concerns to spread throughout the organization, they probably will give rise to additional—and perhaps more serious—concerns later on.

No matter how concerned you may be as the result of a current business reversal, do not let those concerns affect your employees. Address the problem, solve the problem, remove the cause of your concern and move forward according to your basic business plan.

141. Caught off guard

PROBLEM: Too often, companies fail to recognize a crisis in the making. As a result, they are caught off balance and totally unprepared to deal with the situation.

DIAGNOSIS: *Before* a crisis occurs, take the time to look at your business and explore its areas of greatest vulnerability. These are where future crises are likely to occur.

If you know what your weak points are, you can take some very specific steps to prevent crises from occurring—or to minimize the effects if they do occur.

Failure is determined by what you *allow* to happen; success is determined by what you *make* happen.

PRESCRIPTION: Take the time to "audit" your company's weaknesses. To assure objectivity and candor, you may wish to engage an outside firm to handle this audit for you.

Be sure each of the following activities is studied for its vulnerability to rapid, unexpected change, regardless of the cause:

- Cash position.
- Industrial relations.
- Management succession.
- Hostile takeover.
- Public perception.
- Sudden shifts in the market.
- Governmental regulation or deregulation.
- Adverse international events.
- Product failure.

Next, assign priorities to your resources. Rank crises among them according to: a) probability—which ones are most likely to occur; b) severity—which ones would most seriously affect your operation; and c) cost—how much it might cost to prevent a crisis in each category.

Know precisely how much you can afford to expend on a crisis in terms of manpower, money, prestige, market position, and so on.

Candidly assess your ability to handle a crisis, should one occur.

- Do you have a mechanism to detect an emerging crisis at the earliest possible moment?
- Does bad news travel upward as well as downward within your organization?
- Have you formed and trained a crisis management team, and are the members' responsibilities clearly defined?
- Can you marshal your resources, when necessary, to cope with adversity?
- Is your management prepared to deal with surprise, criticism and the sting of exposed failure?
- Is the design of your organization open and flexible?
- Are you prepared to benefit from a crisis once it has passed?
- Do you have a desire to improve and grow?
- Does change occur easily in your company?
- Are you capable of accepting and implementing new ways of doing things?

142. Crisis alert

PROBLEM: The company wasn't caught flat-footed, but there was no way that the threatened crisis could be avoided. Now that it's here, how do we deal with it?

DIAGNOSIS: Beat back the tendency to panic and face the situation in a cool, logical, straightforward fashion.

PRESCRIPTION:

- Realize that leadership is more vital now than ever. Ships in a storm require the strongest hand on the helm. Take charge, quickly and firmly.
- Don't *assume* that you have all of the facts before you. Be sure that you have a thorough understanding of the situation and all of its nuances.

➲ Define the problem as completely as possible, breaking it down into its component parts. If possible, break those parts down into even smaller parts. Sometimes, if a small problem can be corrected, you will discover that the larger problem disappears.

➲ Evaluate all of the options. Go for the most favorable solution first and work backward from there, if necessary.

➲ When you decide to act, move *decisively*. This is no time to vacillate.

➲ Be sure to determine and (eventually) eliminate the cause of the problem in order to prevent a recurrence.

143. Crisis control

PROBLEM: In the midst of a crisis, the entire front office seems to go up for grabs. Well-intended people often jump into situations where they don't belong. Those who need to make important decisions are often missing, engaged in some other work or lacking in information they need to act appropriately.

As a result, the company always seems to be indecisive, which places you in a poor bargaining position and leaves you susceptible to being led, rather than leading.

DIAGNOSIS: Crises will occur. Recognizing that fact, it only makes sense to be ready for them. In many companies, that means creating an internal crisis control center, which can be invaluable as a means of focusing the talents, energies and activities of the organization onto the problem once a crisis actually occurs.

Always remember, however, that avoiding failure is not the same as achieving success.

PRESCRIPTION: If crises occur with any regularity, if the company is large enough or if the company is engaged in work that makes it a target for attack by outside special-interest groups, unions or what-have-you, designating the space for a crisis control center and establishing a responsible team to handle such crises may be advisable.

Features of a crisis control center

➲ Diagrams of installations, organization charts, pictures of key people, information on products and processes, lists of key customers and suppliers, and other potentially pertinent data.

- Accessibility. A place that team members can get to as quickly and conveniently as possible. It should be totally dedicated to crisis management and, therefore, not located in some team member's office. A normal office is filled with distractions. Besides, such a location tends to suggest that the regular occupant of the office has some special status that may not necessarily apply to his or her position on the crisis team.

- Addresses and telephone numbers of all major players, plus information on any outside resources.

- Dedicated telephones, computer terminals, TVs, copying machines, fax machines, blackboards and any other equipment that may be required in case of an emergency.

- Contingency plans, instructions on emergency procedures and similar directives that may have been prepared in advance.

Use of the center prior to a crisis

- Intelligence gathering.
- Assessing pending situations of a potentially critical nature.
- Developing and testing emergency scenarios and procedures.
- Training employees in how to deal with a crisis.
- Investigating emerging crises.

Use of the center during a crisis

- Gathering information.
- Evaluating the situation.
- Assessing the company's options.
- Selecting the action(s) that are to be taken.
- Issuing instructions during the crisis resolution.
- Monitoring the progress of the crisis situation.

Use of the center after a crisis

- Reconstructing the scenario to determine causes, results, actions, remedies, preventatives.
- Designing early-warning systems to monitor future situations.
- Developing new strategies.

144. Learning from a crisis

PROBLEM: Every time you think the business is moving ahead as planned, some unexpected problem arises, creating a new crisis and forcing you to go back to square one.

DIAGNOSIS: Any business crisis can be unnerving because it disrupts the carefully calculated course that you have laid out for yourself and your business.

It can be argued that the original business plan must have been flawed or such crises would not occur, but everyone knows it is impossible to develop a totally fault-free business plan. Businesses do not exist in a vacuum: Market trends change, the cost of supplies changes, state and federal laws change. All of these can have an impact, positively or negatively, upon the viability of your business plan.

Notice that we have said "positively or negatively," because not all crises are necessarily bad. Indeed, some—although temporarily bothersome— may turn out to be very beneficial.

PRESCRIPTION: Before becoming too concerned about an unexpected crisis, study it thoroughly to see if it cannot be used to your advantage. Can the crisis be used, for example, to:

- Gain an edge on your competition?
- Improve your relationship with a supplier?
- Strengthen your position with a customer?
- Enhance your stature with the employees?
- Keep an adversary off balance?
- Bring an important issue to the forefront?
- Incite your organization so that it will be more receptive to needed change?

A crisis under any of these circumstances may prove to be a blessing in disguise.

Crises present opportunities as well as challenges. They allow a company to change much faster and perhaps to a greater degree than it could possibly change under normal circumstances.

Be on the alert to another possible benefit: Unexpected heroes sometimes emerge during a crisis. If they do, be prepared to recognize them, reward them and possibly promote them within your organization.

145. Worst case: a hostile takeover

PROBLEM: You receive a call from the CEO of another company and he says, in effect: "Tomorrow, I plan to inform the SEC of our intention to acquire a large number of your shares for the purpose of an eventual takeover." What should you do?

DIAGNOSIS: Don't panic. Consult with your key employees and advisers to determine whether this is a good move for your company or a bad one.

If the terms of the acquisition are sufficiently attractive, if a merger would provide your company with an opportunity for considerable new growth and if your own position in the new structure will be secure, you might wish to encourage the move.

If, on the other hand, the proposed merger seems ill-advised, then you have no choice but to fight it.

PRESCRIPTION: There is much to do and you will need time to do it. In most cases, a company interested in taking over your firm will not be anxious to engage in a long, costly battle, so time is on your side. When they discover that you are not interested in the merger, that you will fight their attempts at a takeover and that you have the resources to wage a significant campaign against the merger, they may back out.

- ➲ Call the members of your board, tell them what has happened and explain why you are opposed to the proposal.
- ➲ Form a response team and be sure that everyone understands his or her assignment.
- ➲ Get your specialists involved quickly:
  - Legal, including outside legal counsel.
  - Financial, including your investment bankers.
  - Public affairs, including your public relations advisers.

In the meantime, do nothing that will help your competitors. Refuse to meet with them or to let them meet with any other members of your organization.

Inform your public: your shareholders, employees, lenders, suppliers and key customers. Make sure they understand why you think the proposal is a bad one and that you intend to oppose it.

Make use of your business friends. For instance, a cooperative bank might be persuaded to limit the amount of money that it will lend your competitor, making the takeover unaffordable, or it might provide you with enough funding to drive up the price of your stock, making it less attractive to your competitor. Some other company might be persuaded to buy out your competitor, thereby eliminating the cause of your concern.

Create a defense strategy. The first 72 hours are particularly critical. Consider these possible tactics:

- Stagger the terms of your board members.
- Reincorporate the company.
- Change the company's bylaws to discourage the competitor's takeover tactics.
- Repurchase enough shares of your stock to prevent your competitor from gaining a controlling interest.
- Determine what it is about your company that is appealing to your competitor and change it.
- Tender stock to those who are sympathetic to your position on the proposed merger.
- Look for a white knight, who can rescue your company from the takeover.
- If your stock seems to be undervalued, raise it by taking on debt, repurchasing stock or increasing your dividends, making your company less attractive as a takeover candidate.
- Seek out regulatory means of delaying or denying the competitor's intentions.
- Look for legal technicalities that would prevent the takeover.
- Arrange a leveraged buyout.
- Initiate attacks on the competitor.
- Divest the company of its most attractive component(s), thereby making it a less attractive candidate for takeover.
- Investigate the possibility of making a counteroffer by which your company would acquire the competitor, rather than having the competitor acquire you.

146. When hard work isn't enough

PROBLEM: The harder you work, the more you fall behind. You start work earlier and quit later every week, but you still can't seem to catch up.

DIAGNOSIS: Although it may be difficult for you to admit at first, *you* could be the cause of the problem! It's often hard to understand that we can create our own failure. Hard work is always admirable, but it's not always fruitful.

PRESCRIPTION: You must learn to work smarter, not longer or harder. Specifically:

- Develop other "experts" to do some of the things you have been doing. Don't be afraid to delegate.
- Hire people you can trust to make decisions without you.
- Avoid unrealistic deadlines.
- Don't take on more work than you can do well.
- Treat yourself to a break now and then to recharge your batteries and maintain your health.

147. Coping with failure

PROBLEM: After five years in business, you are well short of your original projections. The company has grown, but not as much as you had thought it would. The company is profitable, but your gross is far less than you had hoped. The world has not yet beaten a path to your door. Perhaps someone else could have done better?

DIAGNOSIS: It sounds like you are feeling sorry for yourself and are beginning to feel that you're a failure in your business endeavors. Perhaps you have seen others accomplish *more* with *less*.

Nonetheless, you should realize that your company *has* grown, that it *is* profitable and that there is much more yet to come. As long as you are making progress, there is nothing to be glum about.

PRESCRIPTION: Accept the following truths and apply them to yourself and your own special set of circumstances.

- ⮑ Realize that you are not perfect.
- ⮑ Decide what is most important—avoiding failure or doing something worthwhile.
- ⮑ Recognize that *doing nothing* is the only sure way to avoid failure.
- ⮑ Understand that everyone plays to win, but that there is a loser as well as a winner in every situation. This means that, in any given situation, there's generally a 50-50 chance that you may lose.

With these realizations in mind, try to apply these concepts whenever you contemplate your business ambitions:

- ⮑ Be able to distinguish between a personal failure and a team failure.
- ⮑ Accept failure as a part of the learning process.
- ⮑ Try to win more often than you lose.
- ⮑ Try never to lose in a critical situation.
- ⮑ Analyze each failure to see *what* caused it, not *who*.
- ⮑ Dwell on your successes, not on your failures, and maintain a confident, positive attitude about yourself and about what you are doing.

148. The essential steps in rebuilding

PROBLEM: You have acquired a business that was about to go under, thinking that it would be easier to salvage an established firm than to start from scratch. Subsequently, however, you have learned that there is more to rebuilding a failed company than you had imagined.

DIAGNOSIS: Working to revitalize a failed business usually involves dealing with at least two major groups of people: the company's employees and the company's customers.

The company's employees often feel that they must share some of the responsibility for the failure of the business. As a result, they may feel inept, incapable, unsuccessful, beaten, vulnerable and insecure. The employees need to know that their work is appreciated and important. They need to know that they will be carrying the ball a good deal of the time while you rebuild the company, and that you consider them to be an essential part of the team that eventually will lead the firm back to prosperity.

The company's customers need to know that you understand their needs, that your company has the ability to serve their needs, that you are capable of rebuilding your company and taking care of their needs simultaneously, that you will deal with them honestly and that your company respects and deserves their loyalty.

PRESCRIPTION: Relationships with customers are symbiotic; that is, they develop and prosper because they provide benefits to both parties. As the new owner of a once-successful business, there is little that you must do to perpetuate that relationship beyond upholding your end of the bargain. The same conditions would apply if you were starting a business from scratch.

Restoring the morale and confidence of your employees can be much more difficult, and the more employees there are, the more difficult the task.

One of the most direct methods of accomplishing that task is to empower the employees to help you rebuild the company.

Obviously, major changes must be made; the old approach has failed. If you are to rebuild, you will need new ideas, and there is no better way to learn what is wrong with a company—and how to correct those wrongs—than from those who know the organization best: the employees. The employees not only have the ability to help, but they also have the desire. Both their personal and their professional interests are at stake; everyone wants to be associated with a winner.

When employees actually *recommend* a change, they are far less inclined to *resist* the change and others similarly recommended. Furthermore, they take a great deal of pride in their role as an instrument for revitalizing their firm.

149. Starting with the P&L

PROBLEM: You have acquired a company that is down at the heels and needs to be restructured. The products/services are good and the price structure is competitive. Your share of the market, although it could be better, is sufficient to give you confidence that there is hope for the future.

Is there any guide to help you restructure a business in the most efficient, most expeditious, most productive manner?

DIAGNOSIS: Ultimately, businesses fail for only one reason: They are no longer profitable. Therefore, when a person starts to rebuild a failing business, one of the logical starting points is a review of the latest Profit and Loss (P&L) statement.

PRESCRIPTION: Starting with the P&L statement, determine all of the areas in which the company has been spending money. Decide what individual within the company should be responsible for monitoring the financial condition of that specific function. In some cases, one individual may be responsible for monitoring several different but related functions.

Then set a standard for each function—that is, tell each of the employees responsible for monitoring a given function how much that function has cost, based on an average of several years' experience.

Next, challenge that employee—and any of the personnel who may be under his or her supervision—to suggest ways to reduce the cost and/or increase the productivity of any function(s) for which they are accountable.

Caution: Allow your employees to recommend changes, but not to make changes without prior approval. Cost-cutting is not your only objective. If a cost-cutting proposal results in compromising the quality of your product, for example, it may not be worth pursuing.

Create performance incentives and establish a means by which the employees can monitor their own progress, such as:

- ➲ Provide each responsible employee with a monthly report that compares current performance to last month's—and last year's—performance.

- ➲ If the employee is to receive, let's say, an annual performance-based bonus, let him or her know—in actual dollars and cents—how he or she is progressing to date.

- ➲ If there are comparable components elsewhere in the company (for example, in another plant), let employees know how their performance compares to that of their counterparts.

- ➲ In larger organizations, it usually is beneficial to spread the rewards of good performance among as many employees as possible to encourage maximum participation. Give the annual performance bonus *to the department*, for example, rather than to an individual.

- ➲ Make the reward substantial enough to provide a true incentive. Have you noticed that few people will bother to stoop down to pick up a penny these days?

- ➲ Hold regular meetings regionally or departmentally to discuss the company's progress. Let the employees know that they are largely responsible for that progress. Recognition often can be as effective an incentive as cash; together, they can produce miracles. Let the employees know that you are proud of *them*, and not simply proud of the figures on your P&L.

Chapter 15

Making a new start

150. When it's time to sell the business

PROBLEM: You have decided to sell the business and don't know where to start the process.

DIAGNOSIS: In most cases, this is not a step you should take before consulting an attorney, as well as gathering some information and consulting with specialists.

PRESCRIPTION: To sell your business you will want to: a) locate some potential purchasers; b) be assured of adequate financing; c) negotiate the price and terms of the sale; and d) finalize the transaction.

➲ Begin by preparing a sales memorandum, a document that spells out what is for sale and why someone would want to buy it:

• Describe the business and list its assets.

• Show sales for the past three years and a sales forecast for the current year.

• Describe the customers, staff, plant and equipment involved in the sale.

• Explain why the business is for sale and be candid about it.

• Specify the sales price and the terms.

• Describe your vision of a potential purchaser.

• Give a brief history of the business.

• Specify who an interested party should contact about purchasing the business.

➲ "Due diligence" is the period during which buyer and seller review each other's legal, financial and business documentation. At this time, other documents also will be needed:

- A confidentiality agreement.
- Financial reports specifying what is and what is not included, and why.
- Income and expense statements and projections.
- Cash flow statements and projections.
- Balance sheet and assumptions.
- Lists of fixed assets, inventory, suppliers and customers.
- Such legal documents as leases, contracts, mortgages, loans and insurance policies.
- Federal, state and local tax returns.
- Summaries of any outstanding litigation.
- Copies of your public relations materials—press releases, brochures, etc.
- Biographies of senior management.

Before due diligence begins, both parties should sign a "letter of understanding," which confirms their interest in the sale, the approximate price and terms of the sale, and the time frame for reaching the closing.

The buyer should have the seller deposit funds in an escrow account. In the event the buyer can't get financing or causes delays, the escrow may be released to the seller as a "kill fee."

During the period of due diligence, the seller should investigate the buyer. Try to find out:

- If the buyer can afford the purchase.
- How the buyer will finance the purchase—cash, loan, mortgage or leverage.
- Whether approvals—bank, Small Business Administration, etc.—are needed.
- What the buyer really wants—assets, patents, customers, employees, other.
- How quickly the buyer can close.

As the seller, you must control the timing. Tell the buyer when you expect a commitment and when you need to close.

➲ Closing the deal can depend on the type of financing involved.
- Buying the shares of a corporation is perhaps the easiest form of purchase.

- A company in bankruptcy can still be sold, but the deal should be handled by an experienced attorney.

- Several methods of payment can be used, including lump sum, time payments, time payments followed by a balloon payment, and performance payments.

Any adjustments to the price, terms and agreements regarding the sale are made at the time of closing. Be prepared. Agree in advance on any documents to be exchanged.

151. What's your business worth?

PROBLEM: You have lost confidence in the business you started three years ago. The financials are okay, but you simply don't enjoy the relationships as before. A friend will sell you his business, which you think would suit your skills and interests better, *but* you don't know what your present company is worth.

DIAGNOSIS: You should calculate answers to the following questions before you seriously consider another opportunity. Unless you have this information, you will not know how to compare the value of either the business you now own or the new one.

PRESCRIPTION:

1. Estimate the company's earnings for a 12-month period beginning on the date of valuation. Base that estimate on:

The dollar volume of sales anticipated over the 12 months. From that, subtract the cost of goods and the cost of labor to produce a gross profit estimate for the year.

From the gross profit, subtract the company's total annual operating expenses, which include:

- Sales expense.

- Administrative expense.

- Executive salaries.

- Depreciation (or a replacement fund).

- Cost of maintenance and repairs.

- Miscellaneous or unclassified expenses based upon the previous year's example.

This will give you the company's estimated pretax profit for the year. (Note that it does *not* reflect interest expense, since interest expense can vary. Interest expense will be addressed later.)

2. Determine the value of the company's tangible assets. An experienced appraiser can provide you with a figure that covers:

- Land.
- Buildings.
- Furniture and equipment.
- Inventory.

Add the appraisal value of those assets and to that, add the amount of working capital that will be required for one year's operations.

3. Calculate the "cost of money" or the annual investment cost of the business's tangible assets. This is your substitute for interest expense.

Take the value of the company's tangible assets, calculated in the last step of the equation, and multiply it by an assumed interest rate. For simplicity, use a rate four points above the current inflation rate.

4. Next, determine the company's excess earnings by subtracting its "cost of money" (just computed) as the assumed interest rate from the earnings calculated in the first step.

5. Compute the projected excess earnings—a figure that is appropriate for the particular business being examined. This multiple reflects the risk, stability and other factors associated with the business to show you whether the company is below average, average or above average compared to other companies of comparable size.

Use these categories to "rank" the company in question according to the variables listed:

Risk
0 = Continuity of income at risk
3 = Steady income likely
6 = Growing income assured

Competitiveness
0 = Highly competitive in unstable market
3 = Normal competitive conditions
6 = Little competition in market, high cost of entry for new
    competition

Industry status
0 = Declining industry
3 = Industry growing somewhat faster than inflation
6 = Dynamic industry, rapid growth likely

Track record

0 = Recent startup, not established

3 = Well-established

6 = Long record of sound operation with outstanding reputation

Growth prospects

0 = Business has been declining

3 = Steady growth, slightly faster than the inflation rate

6 = Dynamic growth rate

Image

0 = No status, rough or dirty work

3 = Respected business in satisfactory environment

6 = Challenging business in attractive environment

Add the ratings that you have given the company in each of the six categories and then divide the total by six to obtain an average rating per category. This figure is your "Projected Excess Earnings."

(**Note:** For greatest benefit, use the ratings given here to denote a *range*, rather than an *absolute* figure. In other words, a company that you are evaluating may not be an actual 0 in a particular category, nor a precise 3; but if it is closer to being a 0 than it is to being a 3, give it a rating of 1 in that category.)

6. Calculate the value of the company's excess earnings by multiplying the excess earnings figure determined in step 4 by the multiple computed in step 5.

7. Now you can determine the total value of the business by adding the value of its assets (from step 2) to the value of its excess earnings (from step 6).

You should note that there are a number of areas in which this formula does not work. For example:

- Information businesses are very difficult to value and purchases often are based on an initial payment plus future payments that are calculated on the business' sales and earnings.
- Startups also are very hard to value. Those in fields based on exciting technology may be worth much more than the value of their assets or the prospects for immediate earnings would indicate.

- High-tech businesses are generally valued by the condition of the acquisition market.

- High-leverage businesses have special qualities that make them worth more than a figure based on this formula might indicate.

- "Hobby" businesses actually are part business and part pleasure, hence hard to put a price on.

- Professional businesses, such as law offices, medical practices and accounting businesses, are generally priced according to prevailing practices, based on a percentage of future billings.

This will provide you with a quantitative guide on which to base your asking price or judge the relative worth of one company versus another.

152. Shopping for a bargain

PROBLEM: Sometimes, it seems like every business on the market views itself as the goose that lays the golden egg. When you ask about the sale price, they would like you to believe that they're all the McDonald's or Microsoft of the next generation. Isn't there a way to find some "bargains" when you're in the market to buy a small business?

DIAGNOSIS: It's often much easier to buy an existing business that to start a new one. You acquire an established business with an established clientele, and it's usually possible to grow much faster. But how do you know what to pay for it?

When you're staging a garage sale, you don't tell your customers that all of your shoes have holes in the soles, do you?

Buying a business is similar to buying a house—the owner sets an asking price that is much higher than he or she expects to get for the place, then a potential buyer offers a figure that's much less than the owner is likely to accept and the owner then makes a counteroffer. So it goes until you arrive at a figure that is acceptable to both the seller and the buyer.

PRESCRIPTION: If you're shopping for a business at "bargain prices," you might try one of these approaches:

- Talk to suppliers, competitors, bankers and others who may know when there's a bargain on the market.

- Look for an owner who's ready to retire.

- Watch for bankruptcies.
- Look for businesses that are traditionally late in paying their bills.
- Watch for partners who break up and go their separate ways.
- Be conscious of owners who die, leaving widows who want to sell.
- Wait until there's a weakness in the local economy. When the economy is strong, things tend to be overpriced.

Remember, however, that you often get what you pay for. If a business can be bought for a bargain price, there may be a good reason for it.

Conclusion

Become your own troubleshooter

In these pages, we've presented many solutions to the troubles that plague small businesses. But we are not kidding ourselves. We know we have not anticipated every single problem you will encounter. But this is certain—if you follow these guidelines, you will have a better company tomorrow. You will be better prepared for next week, next month and next year.

The ultimate goal for everyone in business should be to become his or her own troubleshooter. May this be the start you needed to become the best in your field.

Other books by Roger Fritz

What Managers Need to Know (1975)

Productivity and Results (1981)

Rate Yourself As a Manager (1985)

You're In Charge: A Guide for Business and Personal Success (1986)

The Inside Advantage (1986)

Nobody Gets Rich Working for Somebody Else (1987, 1993)

Personal Performance Contracts (1987, 1993)

If They Can—You Can! Lessons from America's New Breed of Successful Entrepreneurs (1988)

Rate Your Executive Potential (1988)

Management Ideas That Work (1989)

Ready, Aim, HIRE! (Coauthor, 1991)

How to Export: Everything You Need to Know to Get Started (1991)

The Entrepreneurial Family: How to Sustain the Vision and Value in Your Family Business (1992)

Think Like a Manager (1992)

Sleep Disorders—America's Hidden Nightmare (1993)

The Sales Manager's High Performance Guide (Editor, 1993)

A Team of Eagles (1994)

How to Manage Your Boss (1994)

Index